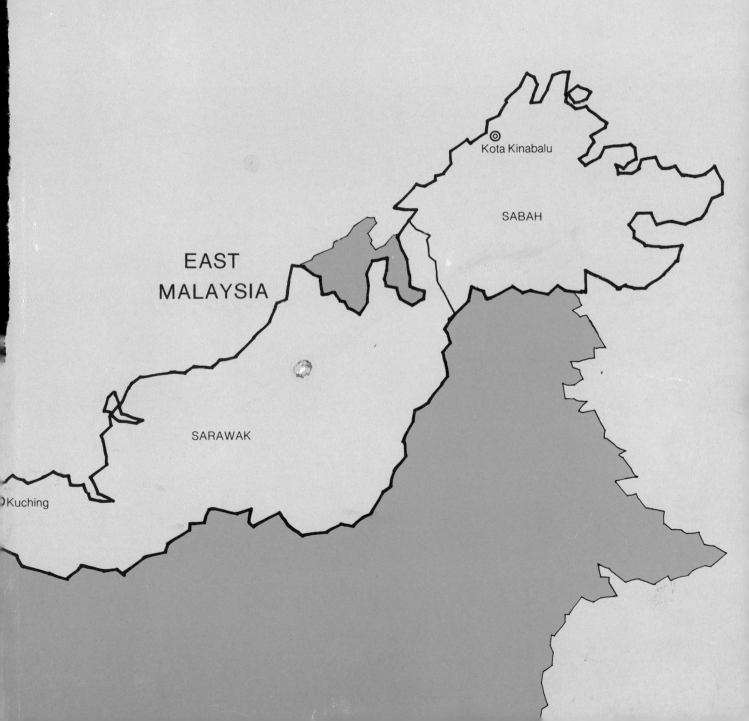

Publisher's Note
East and West Malaysia have been
drawn to different scales. The scale
for East Malaysia is approximately
...
...
...

D0871352

Kota Kinabalu

SABAH

EAST
MALAYSIA

SARAWAK

Kuching

Rasa Malaysia

the complete Malaysian cookbook

Betty Yew

Photographs by Harold Teo

TIMES BOOKS
International

Rasa Malaysia

the complete Malaysian cookbook

Betty Yew

Photographs by

Harold Teo

© 1982 TIMES BOOKS INTERNATIONAL
TIMES CENTRE
1 New Industrial Road
Singapore 1953

078210

Printed in Singapore by
Tien Mah Litho Printing Co (Pte) Ltd

to Peng,
more than ever

Contents

NEGRI SEMBILAN

SELANGOR

Foreword

Malaysia has a worldwide reputation for her almost infinite variety and quality of food and for the incomparable skill of her cooks. This is not a reputation earned consciously; it springs from the inventiveness of our ancestors, from adaptations and improvements made by successive generations of Malaysian cooks who have sought continuously for the key to new flavours and tastes to please our palates. Our reputation has not been built on what fashionable westerners refer to as haute cuisine — the expensive dishes only the privileged can afford. It is derived from traditional recipes, from the countless *kampungs* scattered throughout the length and breadth of Malaysia; this is the food enjoyed by *everyone,* either daily or during special festive occasions in Malaysia.

The traditional skills in food selection, preparation and cooking are part of our multi-cultural heritage, with each culture making its distinctive contribution. Every state has its own specialties and in each there is a great range of variety. It is very important that these skills are not lost as we move into a new international age with many external influences that threaten to change our tastes and habits. In our larger towns we witness the introduction of international restaurants and fast food outlets; to most of us they are a novelty, but soon they will become the norm. We must take care that they do not eventually supplant the dishes for which Malaysia has such a deserved reputation, or cause us to lose our traditional tastes.

It is our good fortune that Mrs Betty Yew has anticipated the need to record our culinary heritage. The publication of her book *Rasa Malaysia* is well timed. It is far more than just another cookery book; it is a historical guide to our Malaysian culinary art. Every state is explored; we learn the origins of the dishes we enjoy so much and how they are traditionally prepared. The book will allow us to share our traditions with each other and with the world outside. And one of our greatest joys is in giving, particularly in giving our traditional Malaysian hospitality.

Haji Mohamed Ishak bin Haji Mohamed Ariff   19 May 1982
SMS, DJN, KMN, PPT, PJK

Preface

Have you ever lived in Malaysia? Stopped over? Perhaps you stay here. A steady rhythm is apparent after a while. It is there in the serenity and languor of the country and suburbs, in the continuity of lifestyle of the rural people—a secure, timeless quality to be savoured in their industry, daily round, not less in their food and the way they serve it.

Malaysian cuisine is rich in its variety, the result of multiracial influences, both past and cosmopolitan present. The blend is exotic: Malay, Chinese, Peranakan, Indian, Eurasian. Yet, paradoxically, there is a unique taste attributable to the distinctive way of cooking in each particular state.

In *Rasa Malaysia*, I shall introduce that intriguing taste peculiar to the various states as we go through some of the Malaysian favourites enjoyed by everyone and traditional specialties gathered firsthand from many dear *makciks* and *neneks*. Their epicurean capabilities, total recall and *agak-agak* culinary skills are rare. The ability of the older generation to lavish tender care in the preparation of their specialties, their enduring patience—these qualities surely deserve emulation.

For easy reference, I have attempted a systematic grouping of states, from south to north of Peninsular Malaysia, and then to East Malaysia. This is not done with any bias in mind and should not be taken as a reflection of the order of importance of any state. Malaysian cities have some of the most varied Eastern and Western cuisines in the nation; a delightful array of provincial cuisine as well as Chinese food is available. For this reason I have included some of the more popular Chinese favourites.

In the process of writing this book, I have derived immense pleasure and satisfaction discovering for myself the infinite possibilities in style and preparation that make cooking a constantly challenging endeavour. Discover this heritage of Malaysian cooking with me. I believe you will find the journey rewarding and enjoyable.

Acknowledgements

I wish to express my gratitude to Puan Asmah Zainuddin, a dedicated cook who captured my interest in Malay cooking, and to many dear friends who contributed generously to my collection of recipes. My deepest appreciation goes to Tuan Haji Mohamed Ishak bin Haji Mohamed Ariff for writing the Foreword.

A special thank you to Mrs Soh Chak Yuen, Mrs Teo Koon Swee, Mr Khoo Choon Boon and Mr Law Teck Soon for their invaluable assistance during the long and hectic photography sessions; to Mrs Margaret Terning, Mrs Dora Degouff, Mrs Ajid Gill, Mrs Pat Sen, Puan Asiah Abidin, Puan Sabaria Roslidi, Puan Masconah Sharif, Puan Siti Rafeah, Puan Siti Fatimah and Mr TS Poh for the loan of their beautiful crockery, tablecloths and other material for photography; particularly to Mr Boo Seng Hock for the loan of Aw pottery; to Mr Harold Teo for his imaginative photography; to Cik Matus Said for translating the manuscript into Bahasa Malaysia; and to my dearest husband, Peng, who as always makes all things possible.

Helpful Hints

Banana Leaves

To soften banana leaves for wrapping *kuih*, either scald in boiling water or pass quickly over flame. If time permits, sun banana leaves for two hours. This gives them a better fragrance.

Bittergourd

Scrape off the white seed portions then soak cut pieces in salt water to lessen its bitter taste.

Black Shrimp Paste

This is sold in plastic jars and is a thick black paste. Like dried shrimp paste (*belacan*) it is made from shrimps and is usually taken straight off the jar diluted with a little warm water.

Blender or Chopper

As far as possible make full use of these time-saving gadgets. The electric chopper does a fine job, even with chilli seeds. If you feel the result is still not fine enough, a grinding stone can be used after blending.

A good liquidizer does an excellent job except with chilli seeds. However, frying the blended ingredients will take a little longer because of the extra water added. Always remember to slice ingredients, especially lemon grass and galingale, before blending, chopping or pounding.

Candlenuts

A hard oily nut available shelled or unshelled. It is used to thicken curry and make it more *lemak*. If not available use cashew nuts as a substitute.

Cloud Ear Fungus

This is black and dried in form and not an expensive ingredient. It has to be soaked to soften before use.

Coconut Residue

When *pati santan* is cooked over low heat, stirring constantly for quite some time, it thickens and eventually oil separates, leaving a residue. Drained from oil, this residue is crisp and rich brown. It is used in desserts or sambals.

Cummin and Fennel

Cummin is smaller and darker than fennel seeds. Both are essential ingredients in most curries, but cummin is usually used in smaller quantities than fennel.

Curry Powder

If a recipe calls for curry powder for the various meats, use your favourite brand. However, ensure it is fresh and fragrant and remember to mix with a little water before frying to prevent it from sticking to the pan. If it does stick before being well fried, sprinkle in a little water.

Double Lime Leaf

The Chinese name for this unique fragrant leaf is horrendous. *Fat fong kum yip* literally means 'leper leaf' and the name is probably due to the rough, stubbly skin of the fruit. The leaf has a double petal and is used commonly in curries and Malay *rendang*.

Fresh Chicken Stock

Stock obtained from boiling the bony parts of chicken like the claws, wing tips, neck, etc. in water over low heat.

Ground Ingredients of Mixed Spices

A good non-stick pan is ideal for frying these as the ingredients have to be fried over low heat until fragrant and a film of oil appears on the surface. Ground ingredients can always be prepared in advance and frozen in airtight containers to be used when required.

Kerisik

Grated coconut, pan-fried without oil over low heat until brown and pounded or blended to a fine paste. This can be frozen for as long as two weeks.

Lemon Grass

A tall grass that grows quite easily in clumps. Discard the leaves and use about 10-12 cm (4-5 in) from the thick root end. For grinding, the outer layer is usually removed before use. When a recipe calls for lightly crushed lemon grass, smash lightly with a pestle or the flat surface of a cleaver.

Local Beef

If it is not one of the tender cuts, score meat lightly with the blunt edge of a cleaver. Meat should always be cut across the grain.

Palm Sugar

A dark brown sugar which comes wrapped in dried leaves in cylindrical or round cake form. It is made from the sap of coconut palm flowers and has a lovely fragrance. To melt palm sugar, chop into smaller pieces. When it melts into syrup, strain to remove grit.

Roasted Peanuts

Made from shelled raw peanuts and pan-fried dry over low heat, stirring constantly until golden brown. Rub the thin brown skin then winnow in a flat tray or basket. After cooling, they store well in an airtight container in the refrigerator.

Screwpine Leaves

Dark green in colour, they are used for their special fragrance. *Kuih* and especially sweets made with coconut milk simply will not be the same without these aromatic leaves.

Seasoning a New Earthen Pot

Soak the earthen pot in water, preferably overnight. Put in a whole coconut, grated, and fry over low heat until coconut is dry and brown. Discard coconut and rinse the pot.

Shallot Crisps or Crispy Shallots

Slice shallots thinly crosswise. Heat enough oil for deep-frying and stir shallots over low heat until pale brown. Remove with a perforated ladle and drain on absorbent paper. When cool, store in an airtight container. Shallot crisps keep well for several weeks in the refrigerator. (Garlic crisps are prepared the same way.)

Thick and Thin Coconut Milk

Thick coconut milk is the first extraction of milk from grated coconut after adding a little water. Thin coconut milk is the second extraction of milk after adding more water. *Pati santan* is coconut milk extracted without adding water. The best way to do this is by squeezing the grated coconut, a little at a time, in a piece of fine muslin cloth.

Grated coconut kept in the refrigerator or freezer will not yield as much as freshly grated coconut. Ideally, extract the required amount of milk, add a pinch of salt, *then* freeze. Frozen this way, it can be kept for as long as a week. However, if you do not have the time to extract milk before freezing, thaw frozen grated coconut and add hot water instead.

Wild Ginger Flower

Usually not a flower but a bud from a wild ginger plant. The tall plant resembles the galingale plant and the bud has a lovely fragrance. Do not discard the stem, but use by smashing lightly with the flat surface of a cleaver to get full fragrance.

Weights and Measures

Metric and imperial measures are used throughout this book. All measures are level except when stated otherwise. However, measures for liquids do not have to be adhered to precisely as different cookers vary in heat intensity. A little extra liquid can be added, for instance, if meat is not properly cooked. Quantities for salt or sugar can be changed according to individual taste.

Cup Equivalents

1 cup cooking oil or liquid	250 ml	
2 cups cooking oil or liquid	500 ml	
6 tablespoons cooking oil or liquid	½ cup	
12 tablespoons cooking oil or liquid	1 cup	
1 cup plain flour	120 g	4 oz
1 cup sugar	240 g	8 oz
1 cup rice	240 g	8 oz
1 tablespoon flour	30 g	1 oz
1 rounded tablespoon sugar	30 g	1 oz

Oven Temperatures

	°C	°F	Gas Regulo
Moderate	175	350	6
Hot	205	400	8
Very hot	220	425	9

JOHORE

Occupying the entire southern portion of the Malay peninsula, rich with pineapple plantations and oil palm and rubber estates, is Johore State. Johore Bahru, its modern capital city, is situated at the southernmost tip and is connected to Singapore island by a busy causeway.

Johore has a strong Malay culture and Malay cuisine is interestingly varied with a taste of Javanese. Laksa Johore or Laksa Bersantan, Mee Rebus and Sayur Lodeh, an enticing mixed vegetable curry, are some of the tempting favourites to match healthy appetites.

The Chinese population in Johore is mainly Teochew and some of their popular offerings are Teochew Duck, Five-Spice Meat Rolls and Steamed Fish Teochew Style. Teochew cooking is generously spiced with five-spice powder and is renowned for its variety of braised meats in dark soy sauce, normally eaten with bland porridge or flat rice noodles.

Opposite: Syrup Bandung and Kuih Koleh-koleh Kacang

Ikan Masam Manis

Preparation: 10 minutes   Cooking: 25 minutes

600 g (1⅓ lb) black pomfret
2 tablespoons flour
½ teaspoon pepper ⎫
½ teaspoon salt   ⎬ *combined*
2 tablespoons water ⎭
oil for deep-frying
3 shallots, sliced
2 cloves garlic, sliced
2½ cm (1 in) ginger, cut into strips
1 cup water
½ small carrot, cut into 4 cm
  (1½ in) strips
2 red chillies, seeded and cut into strips
2 dessertspoons light soy sauce ⎫
2 dessertspoons vinegar   ⎪
1 teaspoon sugar   ⎪
¼ teaspoon monosodium   ⎬ *combined*
  glutamate   ⎪
½ teaspoon salt   ⎪
1 teaspoon cornflour   ⎭
coriander leaves

Wash fish and make two slits across on each side. Coat with combined flour batter and deep-fry in hot oil until light brown and crisp. Drain and place fish on a serving dish.

Remove oil, leaving 2 tablespoonfuls in the *kuali*. Fry shallots, garlic and ginger until fragrant then add water. When it comes to a boil put in carrot and chillies. Simmer for 5 minutes then add remaining seasoning.

Pour hot gravy on top of fish and garnish if desired with coriander leaves.

Sambal Ikan with Belimbing

Preparation: 10 minutes   Cooking: 15 minutes

450 g (1 lb) spanish mackerel, preferably
  head portion
1 teaspoon salt
8 small sour starfruit
¼ teaspoon salt
3 tablespoons oil

Ground Ingredients
6 red chillies, seeded
10 dried chillies, soaked
10 shallots
3 candlenuts
2½ x 1¼ cm (1 x ½ in) dried shrimp paste

2 red chillies, seeded and sliced at a slant
1 stalk lemon grass, crushed
½ coconut, grated (for 2 cups coconut
  milk)
1 teaspoon sugar
½ teaspoon salt

Season fish with salt for 10 minutes. Rub small sour starfruit with salt and leave aside.

Heat oil in a *kuali* and fry ground ingredients, sliced chillies and lemon grass until fragrant and oil separates.

Put in coconut milk, small sour starfruit, sugar and salt and bring to a slow boil. Put in fish and simmer for 5 minutes until cooked.

Note: Small sour starfruit is green in colour and usually the size of a thumb. If not available use a tablespoon of lemon juice as substitute.

Gulai Ikan Pedas

Preparation: 15 minutes   Cooking: 15 minutes

600 g (1⅓ lb) wolf herring, cut into
   7½ cm (3 in) slices
1 teaspoon salt
5 tablespoons oil
5 shallots ⎤
3 cloves garlic ⎦ *sliced*

Ground Ingredients
30 dried chillies, soaked
5 shallots
3 cloves garlic
2½ cm (1 in) ginger
1¼ cm (½ in) square dried shrimp paste
1 teaspoon turmeric powder

2 tablespoons tamarind paste ⎤ *mixed and*
3 cups water ⎦ *strained*
180 g (6 oz) salted Tientsin cabbage,
   sliced and soaked
½ teaspoon salt, or to taste
1 teaspoon sugar
½ teaspoon monosodium glutamate

Clean fish, rub with salt and leave aside.

Heat oil in a *kuali* and lightly brown shallots and garlic. Add ground ingredients and fry till fragrant. Add strained tamarind juice and bring to a boil.

Put in salted Tientsin cabbage and simmer for 2 minutes. Add salt, sugar, monosodium glutamate and fish and cook till fish is done.

Panggang Ikan Terubuk

Preparation: 10 minutes Grilling: 20 minutes

600 g (1⅓ lb) shad
½ teaspoon salt
oil

Chilli Tamarind Sauce
15-20 bird chillies, ground
5 shallots, sliced
1 teaspoon sugar
2 teaspoons
   tamarind paste ⎤ *mixed and*
3 tablespoons   *strained*
   water ⎦
¼ teaspoon salt, or to taste
} *combined*

Wash the fish, remove entrails but not the scales. Rub body cavity with salt and brush with oil.

Grill fish over glowing coals or under a preheated grill. (If grilling, line tray with foil.) Grill fish 10 minutes on each side, brushing with more oil.

Serve hot with Chilli Tamarind Sauce as a dip.

Note: Ikan terubuk is full of fine bones and has a special flavour of its own. Keeping the scales when grilling or pan-frying this fish helps to impart and preserve that special flavour.

Otak Otak Tenggiri

Preparation: 25 minutes   Cooking: 20 minutes   Makes: 16 packets

600 g (1⅓ lb) spanish mackerel,
 central portion
1 teaspoon salt
5 eggs

Ground Ingredients
15 dried chillies, soaked
10 bird chillies
5 shallots
2 cloves garlic
2 stalks lemon grass
3 slices galingale
1¼ cm (½ in) square dried
 shrimp paste
1 teaspoon turmeric powder

3 double lime leaves
2 turmeric leaves   *sliced finely*
20 'kaduk' leaves
1 coconut, grated (for 1 cup thick coconut
 milk)
2 teaspoons salt
½ teaspoon monosodium glutamate
banana leaves

Wash and cut the fish into two halves, then cut into 5 x 4 cm (2 x 1½ in) pieces. Season fish with salt and leave for 15 minutes.

Beat eggs lightly with a fork and stir in ground ingredients and finely sliced leaves. Mix with coconut milk, salt and monosodium glutamate.

Run banana leaves over flame or a heated electric stove until softened, then cut into approximately 15 x 18 cm (6 x 7 in) pieces. Make sure there are no holes or slits in the leaves or gravy will seep through. Wash and dry leaves.

Put a piece of fish in the centre of each piece of leaf. Fold into half then fold one end as illustrated. Put in 2 tablespoons of egg mixture and fold the other end. Fasten with a small piece of satay stick or toothpick. Trim the top neatly with scissors and steam for 20 minutes.

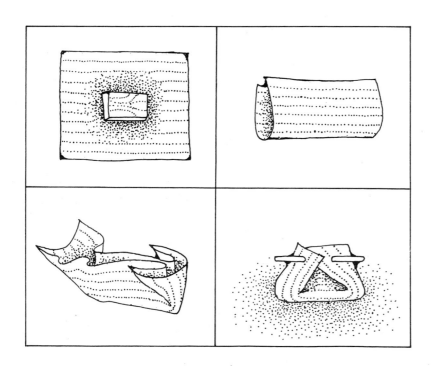

Teochew Steamed Fish

Preparation: 15 minutes   Steaming: 15 minutes   Cooking: 3 minutes

600-900 g (1⅓-2 lb) fish, preferably
   threadfin or pomfret
1½ teaspoons salt
1 teaspoon pepper
120 g (4 oz) salted Tientsin cabbage,
   soaked in water and sliced
4 dried Chinese mushrooms, soaked until
   soft and cut into strips
90 g (3 oz) chicken or pork, cut into strips
4 cm (1½ in) ginger, cut into strips
2 red chillies, cut into strips
2 pickled sour plums
1 teaspoon sesame oil
½ cup water
3 tablespoons oil
3-4 shallots, sliced
2 stalks spring onion | *cut into 5 cm*
2 sprigs coriander leaves | *(2 in) lengths*

Clean fish thoroughly and rub with salt and pepper. Place on a heatproof dish. Spread salted Tientsin cabbage, mushrooms, chicken or pork, ginger and chillies over fish. Lightly squeeze sour plums and place beside fish. Add sesame oil and water.

Place dish in a steamer over rapidly boiling water and steam for 15 minutes.

Meanwhile, heat oil in a *kuali* and fry shallots until lightly browned.

When fish is cooked, pour oil and shallots over fish. Serve garnished with spring onions and coriander leaves.

Sotong Masak Hitam

Preparation: 20 minutes   Cooking: 15 minutes

600 g (1⅓ lb) small-medium cuttlefish
1 teaspoon salt
2 tablespoons oil

Ground Ingredients
5 shallots
3 cloves garlic | *ground*
2½ cm (1 in) turmeric root | *coarsely*
2½ cm (1 in) ginger

2 onions, sliced into rings
2 red chillies, seeded and sliced
1 teaspoon salt
½ teaspoon monosodium glutamate

Wash cuttlefish, remove the entrails and black ink pouch. Keep whole and leave the eyes intact. Rub with salt and leave aside for 15 minutes.

Heat oil in a *kuali* and fry ground ingredients until fragrant. Put in cuttlefish and simmer over low heat for 10 minutes.

Add sliced onions, red chillies, salt and monosodium glutamate. Stir-fry for 2-3 minutes.

Note: This dish may look unappetisingly black but it is sedap *when taken with rice.*

Kari Kambing

Preparation: 15 minutes   Cooking: 1 hour

600 g (1⅓ lb) mutton or beef
7 tablespoons oil
2½ cm (1 in) stick cinnamon
3 cardamoms
6 cloves
2 sections of a star anise

Ground Ingredients
8 shallots
3 cloves garlic   ⎫
5 cm (2 in) ginger   ⎬ combined
2½ cm (1 in) galingale   ⎬
5 tablespoons meat curry   ⎭
   powder

1 coconut, grated (for 2 cups thick
   coconut milk and 3 cups thin
   coconut milk)
4 potatoes, quartered
3 tomatoes, halved
1½ teaspoons salt
½ teaspoon monosodium glutamate

Cut mutton or beef into thin slices.

Heat oil in a pot and fry whole spices for a few minutes. Add curry paste mixture and fry until fragrant and oil separates. Put in meat and fry until meat is well coated with ground ingredients.

Add thin coconut milk and bring to a boil. Then simmer gently for 40 minutes or until meat is almost tender. Put in potatoes, then tomatoes. Add thick coconut milk and simmer until meat is tender and gravy is thick. Add salt and monosodium glutamate.

Satay Daging

(photograph opposite)

Preparation: 1 hour   Grilling: 45 minutes   Makes: 85-90 sticks

1 kg (2⅕ lb) beef

Ground Ingredients
4 stalks lemon grass, sliced ⎫
4 cm (1½ in) turmeric root ⎬ ground
1 teaspoon fennel   ⎬ finely
¾ teaspoon cummin   ⎭

6 heaped teaspoons sugar
1½ tablespoons light soy sauce
3 teaspoons salt
½ teaspoon monosodium glutamate
2 tablespoons oil
85-90 satay sticks or skewers,
   soaked in water
1 stalk lemon grass, crushed at the thicker
   end for basting
1 coconut, grated   ⎫
   (for 'pati santan')   ⎬ combined
4 tablespoons oil   ⎭

Ask the butcher for a tender cut for Satay. Slice meat into 2 x 4 cm (³/₄ x 1½ in) pieces, about 6 mm (¼ in) thick.

Marinate meat with ground ingredients, sugar, light soy sauce, salt, monosodium glutamate and oil for at least 2 hours.

Thread meat onto 7½ cm (3 in) of the satay sticks. Using the crushed lemon grass as a brush, brush meat with combined *pati santan* and oil.

Grill over glowing coal on both sides, basting with *pati santan* and oil mixture several times until meat is well done.

Serve hot with Satay Peanut Sauce, *ketupat* or *nasi himpit* (compressed rice cakes) and cucumber and onion wedges.

Opposite: Satay Daging and Satay Ayam

Satay Ayam

(photograph on page 7)

Preparation: 40 minutes   Grilling: 25-30 minutes   Makes: 30-35 sticks

**600 g (1⅓ lb) chicken meat (from 1
  medium chicken or 4 drumsticks)**

Ground Ingredients
3 stalks lemon grass, sliced
2½ cm (1 in) turmeric root⎫ *ground finely*
2 cloves garlic⎭

2 teaspoons salt
4 heaped teaspoons sugar
1 tablespoon light soy sauce
1 tablespoon oil
**30-35 satay sticks or skewers,
  soaked in water**
**1 stalk lemon grass, crushed at the thicker
  end for basting**
**½ coconut, grated
  (for 'pati santan')**⎫ *combined*
2 tablespoons oil⎭

Slice chicken into 1¼ x 2½ cm (½ x 1 in) pieces. Season with ground ingredients, salt, sugar, light soy sauce and oil and leave for 2 hours.

Thread onto satay sticks or skewers and grill as for Satay Daging (page 6).

Serve hot with Satay Peanut Sauce, *ketupat* or *nasi himpit* (compressed rice cakes) and cucumber and onion wedges.

Note: Soaking satay sticks or skewers in water for a couple of hours prevents the ends from burning during grilling.

Satay Peanut Sauce

(photograph on page 7)

Preparation: 30 minutes   Cooking: 20 minutes

5 tablespoons oil

Ground Ingredients
15 dried chillies, seeded
2 cloves garlic
12 shallots
1 stalk lemon grass, sliced
1 tablespoon coriander⎫ *ground*
1 teaspoon fennel⎪ *finely*
¾ teaspoon cummin⎪
5 candlenuts⎪
**1¼ cm (½ in) square dried
  shrimp paste**⎭

**180 g (6 oz) roasted peanuts, ground
  coarsely**
**1 coconut, grated (for 1½ cups thick
  coconut milk)**
2 teaspoons tamarind paste⎫ *mixed and*
½ cup water⎭ *strained*
2 teaspoons sugar
1½ teaspoons salt

Heat 5 tablespoons oil in a *kuali* and fry ground ingredients until fragrant and oil separates. Put in ground peanuts and thick coconut milk. Bring to a slow boil then add tamarind juice, sugar and salt. Simmer for 5 minutes.

Note: Kajang Satay might be better known for its sauce, but Johore Satay is second to none in its preparation.

Kurma Ayam

Preparation: 15 minutes   Cooking: 40 minutes

1½ kg (3⅓ lb) chicken, cut into 4 large
    pieces
1 teaspoon salt
8 tablespoons oil
125 g (4 oz) kurma curry powder, mixed
    into a paste with water

Ground Ingredients
1 heaped dessertspoon poppy seeds
10 shallots
4 cloves garlic
5 cm (2 in) ginger

3 cups water
4 tablespoons evaporated milk
4 potatoes, halved
2 onions, quartered
small bunch of coriander leaves, cut into
    5 cm (2 in) lengths
4 tomatoes, halved
1½ teaspoons salt
½ teaspoon monosodium glutamate
2 red chillies, split lengthwise
1 tablespoon peas, boiled

Season chicken with salt.

Heat oil in a pot and fry combined curry paste and ground ingredients until fragrant and oil separates.

Add 3 cups water and bring to a slow boil. Put in chicken and simmer over moderate heat, covered, for 15 minutes. Uncover, add evaporated milk, potatoes and onions and simmer until cooked and gravy is thick.

Put in coriander leaves, tomatoes, salt and mono-sodium glutamate.

Serve garnished with red chillies and peas.

Teochew Duck

Preparation: 10 minutes   Cooking: 50 minutes

1½ kg (3⅓ lb) young duck
2 dessertspoons salt, to rub inside duck
1 dessertspoon salt, to rub outside duck
1 tablespoon five-spice powder
150 g (5 oz) galingale, sliced
½ tablespoon oil
1 heaped tablespoon sugar
3 cups water
3 cloves garlic
7½ cm (3 in) stick cinnamon
8 Sichuan peppercorns
4 tablespoons dark soy sauce
1 teaspoon monosodium glutamate

Rub the inside and outside of duck with salt and five-spice powder. Stuff duck with sliced galingale.

Heat oil in a *kuali,* put in sugar and when it turns dark golden in colour add water. Bring to a boil, then put in garlic, spices, dark soy sauce and monosodium glutamate.

Put in duck and add enough water to cover three-quarters of duck. Simmer duck, covered, for approximately 45 minutes until tender and sauce is dark and thick.

Cut duck into serving size pieces and pour sauce over.

Sayur Lodeh

(photograph opposite)

Preparation: 20 minutes Cooking: 20 minutes

7 tablespoons oil

Ground Ingredients
15 red chillies
12 shallots
2 cloves garlic
2½ cm (1 in) dried shrimp paste
5 candlenuts
1 teaspoon turmeric powder

120 g (4 oz) dried prawns, ground
separately
1 coconut, grated (for 1 cup thick coconut
milk and 4 cups thin coconut milk)
1 carrot, cut into 1¼ x 4 cm (½ x 1½ in)
strips
360 g (12 oz) turnip, cut into 1¼ x 4 cm
(½ x 1½ in) strips
4-5 leaves cabbage, cut into 4 cm (1½ in)
pieces
2 eggplants, cut into 1¼ cm (½ in)
thick slices, at a slant
8 long beans, cut into 4 cm (1½ in) lengths
2 firm soybean cakes, cut into small cubes
2 teaspoons salt
½ teaspoon monosodium glutamate

Heat oil in a *kuali* and fry ground ingredients until fragrant. Put in dried prawns and after a few minutes add a little of the thick coconut milk to prevent ground ingredients from sticking to pan. Fry until fragrant.

Put in thin coconut milk and bring to a boil. Add vegetables and soybean cakes. When gravy comes to a boil again, lower heat and simmer till vegetables are soft.

Add remaining thick coconut milk, salt to taste and monosodium glutamate.

Opposite: Sayur Lodeh

Rojak Suun

Preparation: 30 minutes   Cooking: 15 minutes

300 g (10 oz) transparent noodles
300 g (10 oz) beansprouts
600 g (1⅓ lb) potatoes
oil for deep-frying
5 firm soybean cakes
3 cucumbers, sliced
2 small bunches lettuce

Ground Ingredients
15 dried chillies, soaked
150 g (5 oz) dried prawns, washed, dried
  and toasted
1 tablespoon sesame seeds, toasted
3 cloves garlic

2 teaspoons salt
1 tablespoon vinegar
2 teaspoons sugar

Scald transparent noodles, then beansprouts in boiling water. Drain.

Boil potatoes until cooked, then peel and cut into small cubes. Heat oil and deep-fry soybean cakes until light brown in colour. Cut into halves then slice.

Combine transparent noodles, beansprouts, potatoes, soybean cakes and cucumbers in a bowl then place in a dish garnished with lettuce leaves.

Just before serving combine ground ingredients with salt, vinegar and sugar. Mix well and pour over vegetables.

Rojak Tauhu

Preparation: 15 minutes   Cooking: 20 minutes

3 tablespoons oil
300 g (10 oz) raw shelled peanuts
oil for deep-frying
5-6 firm soybean cakes
240 g (8 oz) beansprouts, tailed
  and scalded
2 cucumbers, peeled and cut into small
  wedges

Rojak Sauce
35 bird chillies
2 teaspoons garlic flakes } *ground*
60 g (2 oz) palm sugar, chopped
8 small limes
1¼ cups water
1 tablespoon sugar
1 teaspoon salt

Heat 3 tablespoons oil in a *kuali* and fry peanuts until light golden in colour. Drain from oil, cool then rub to separate skin. Pound peanuts coarsely and leave aside.

Heat oil and deep-fry soybean cakes until lightly browned on both sides. Drain, cool and cut into small cubes.

Combine scalded beansprouts, cucumber wedges and fried soybean cubes in a dish. Just before serving, pour rojak sauce over vegetables.

Rojak Sauce
Combine ground peanuts, ground bird chillies and garlic flakes and palm sugar in a mixing bowl. Squeeze in lime juice through a strainer, mix well and add water, sugar and salt. Stir well.

Sambal Goreng Tempe

Preparation: 20 minutes   Cooking: 25 minutes

4 pieces preserved soybean cake
oil for deep-frying
4 firm soybean cakes
45 g (1½ oz) transparent noodles
450 g (1 lb) prawns, shelled and
   deveined
½ teaspoon salt
4 tablespoons oil
1 large onion, sliced

Ground Ingredients
15 dried chillies, soaked
15 shallots
5 cloves garlic
2½ cm (1 in) turmeric root
2½ x 1¼ cm (1 x ½ in) dried shrimp
   paste

2 red chillies | *seeded and sliced*
2 green chillies | *at a slant*
1 heaped teaspoon tamarind paste | *mixed and*
¼ cup water | *strained*
1 coconut, grated (for 3 cups
   coconut milk)
150 g (5 oz) long beans, cut into
   4 cm (1½ in) lengths
1½ teaspoons salt

Cut preserved soybean cake into 2½ cm (1 in) pieces and deep-fry in hot oil until lightly browned. Remove and drain.

Cut each firm soybean cake into four pieces and deep-fry. Remove and drain.

Wash transparent noodles, drain and deep-fry. Remove and drain. Season prawns with salt and leave aside.

Heat 4 tablespoons oil in a *kuali* and brown sliced onion. Add ground ingredients and chillies and fry until fragrant and oil separates.

Put in prawns and stir-fry for 2 minutes then add strained tamarind juice and coconut milk. Bring to a slow boil, then add long beans, preserved and firm soybean cakes and transparent noodles. Simmer over low heat until long beans are cooked. Season with salt.

Serve with rice.

Note: Tempe *comes in rectangular packets and are easily available at Malay stalls in markets. They are usually wrapped in banana leaves or* daun ketapang. *When fresh from the market they can be kept in the refrigerator for 2-3 days. When they are not fresh they turn a mouldy black.*

Acar Rampai

Preparation: 15 minutes   Cooking: 12 minutes

**2 cucumbers, seed portions discarded,
  cut into 4 cm x 6 mm (1½ x ¼ in) strips**
**1 large carrot, cut into 4 cm x 6 mm
  (1½ x ¼ in) strips**
**2 tablespoons dried radish, washed
  and chopped**
10 shallots, halved
6 cloves garlic, halved
4 red chillies | *seeded and cut*
4 green chillies | *into strips*
150 g (5 oz) ginger, shredded
½ dessertspoon table salt
½ dessertspoon sugar
1 teaspoon turmeric powder
**1 dessertspoon mustard seeds,
  washed and drained**
5 tablespoons oil
4 shallots, sliced
20 dried chillies } *ground*
2½ cm (1 in) turmeric root
½ cup vinegar
¼ cup water
1 dessertspoon sugar } *combined*
¼ teaspoon salt
**½ teaspoon monosodium
  glutamate**
1 tablespoon sultanas

Put cucumbers, carrot, dried radish, shallots, garlic, chillies and ginger into a mixing bowl. Mix well with salt, sugar and turmeric powder and leave for 1 hour. Drain well.

Heat a *kuali* and without adding oil, fry mustard seeds for a minute. Remove and leave aside.

Add oil and when hot, lightly brown sliced shallots and fry ground ingredients until oil separates. Put in vinegar mixture and bring to a boil. Simmer gently for 3 minutes, then put in vegetables, mustard seeds and sultanas.

Note: If short of time, put vegetables in a piece of cloth and squeeze lightly to remove vegetable juice.

Acar Timun

Preparation: 15 minutes   Cooking: 8 minutes

3 cucumbers, peeled and shredded
   coarsely
1 carrot, shredded coarsely
15 shallots, sliced
5 cm (2 in) ginger, shredded
3 red chillies, sliced at a slant
1 tablespoon salt
1 tablespoon garlic flakes,
   crushed lightly
3 tablespoons oil
12 dried chillies, soaked and
   ground
1 teaspoon turmeric powder
3 tablespoons tomato sauce
1 tablespoon water
3 dessertspoons sugar
2 dessertspoons vinegar   } combined
1 teaspoon salt
1 teaspoon monosodium
   glutamate

Combine shredded cucumbers, carrot, shallots, ginger and chillies and mix well with salt. Wrap in a piece of fine muslin cloth and place a heavy weight on top. Leave overnight. Vegetables will be very crisp when water drains away the next day. Remove from cloth and stir in garlic flakes.

Heat oil in a *kuali* and fry ground chillies and turmeric powder for 3 minutes. Put in combined ingredients. When it comes to a boil, add shredded vegetables and stir-fry to mix well for 1 minute. Serve as an accompaniment to Nasi Minyak (below).

Note: If you have forgotten to prepare vegetables overnight, put them in a piece of muslin cloth and squeeze lightly to remove vegetable juice. Garlic flakes are available in most Chinese sundry shops.

Nasi Minyak

Preparation: 15 minutes   Cooking: 30 minutes

3½ kg (7³/₄ lb) Siamese rice
6 tablespoons ghee
7 shallots
4 cloves garlic   } sliced
5 cm (2 in) ginger, shredded
8 cloves
4 cardamoms
2½ cm (1 in) stick cinnamon
7½ cups water
1 small can (170 g/6 oz) evaporated milk
1 tablespoon salt
3 stalks Chinese celery, cut into
   2½ cm (1 in) lengths

Wash rice, drain and put into a rice cooker.

Heat ghee in a *kuali,* lightly brown shallots, garlic and ginger. Put in spices and fry for 2 minutes till fragrant. Add water, evaporated milk and salt and bring to a boil. Add Chinese celery and pour the whole mixture into the rice cooker. Cook till rice is done. Serve hot with meat and fish curries accompanied with a plain mixed vegetable salad or Acar Timun (above).

Note: To make Nasi Biryani, follow the same recipe but use Biryani rice instead of Siamese rice, and add a few sprigs of mint leaves with Chinese celery. When rice is boiling and half-cooked, stir in a few drops of yellow colouring or a few saffron strands mixed with a little milk.

Soto Ayam

(photograph opposite)

Preparation: 45 minutes Cooking: (Rice) 30 minutes (25 Burgers) 20 minutes (Soup) 45 minutes

Rice Cakes/Nasi Himpit
600 g (1⅓ lb) rice
4¼ cups water
pinch of salt

Beef Burgers
600 g (1⅓ lb) potatoes, boiled and mashed
300 g (10 oz) beef, minced
1 tablespoon pepper
1½ teaspoons salt
10 shallots, sliced and browned lightly in
   oil
2 eggs, beaten
a little flour
oil for shallow frying

Chicken Soup
7½ cm (3 in) stick cinnamon
5 sections of a star anise
2 cardamoms
10 black peppercorns
1 heaped teaspoon white peppercorns
1 teaspoon coriander
½ teaspoon fennel
½ teaspoon cummin
15 cups water
5 cm (2 in) ginger, crushed lightly
4 cloves garlic
1½ kg (3⅓ lb) chicken, halved
2 teaspoons salt
1 teaspoon monosodium glutamate
2 tablespoons oil reserved from frying
   shallots (see below)
450 g (1 lb) beansprouts, tailed and scalded
   in boiling water for 1 minute
300 g (10 oz) shallots, sliced and fried crisp
   in oil (reserve 2 tablespoons of this oil)
4 sprigs Chinese celery, chopped
40 bird chillies, ground
3 tablespoons light soy sauce } combined

Rice Cakes/Nasi Himpit
Wash rice, drain and put in a rice cooker. Add water and salt and cook till rice is done. Stir and mash with a wooden spoon while it is still hot. Transfer to a 25 x 15 cm (10 x 6 in) rectangular dish or tin with a flat lid a little bit smaller than the dish or tin. Press lid firmly onto rice and place a heavy object on top to compress rice. Leave overnight in the refrigerator. Cut into 2½ cm (1 in) cubes and leave aside.

Beef Burgers
Put potatoes and minced beef in a bowl and mix well with pepper, salt and fried shallots. Stir in eggs. Form mixture into 5 cm (2 in) diameter patties with wetted hands. Roll lightly in a little plain flour and shallow fry in a little oil for about 5 minutes or until cooked. When cool, quarter each burger.

Chicken Soup
Tie up spices in a piece of clean cloth with thick string. Crush the little bag of spices lightly with a pestle. Prick bag with a skewer.

Put 15 cups of water, the bag of spices, ginger and garlic in a large pot and bring to a slow boil. Put in chicken and simmer, covered, for 30 minutes or until chicken is tender. Add salt and monosodium glutamate. Remove scum from soup and add 2 tablespoons of oil reserved from frying shallots. Remove chicken and tear meat into small pieces. Place in a serving dish.

To Serve Soto Ayam
Put a few rice cubes, some beansprouts, burgers and chicken in a serving bowl. Top with hot chicken soup and garnish with shallot crisps and Chinese celery. Serve hot, and if desired, with a small dish of bird chillies and light soy sauce.

Opposite: Soto Ayam

Nasi Dhal Berhias

Preparation: 15 minutes Cooking: 25 minutes

600 g (1⅓ lb) Siamese rice
300 g (10 oz) lentils, soaked
   (preferably overnight)
1 tablespoon oil
1 tablespoon ghee
2 onions
2½ cm (1 in) ginger } chopped
5 cloves
2½ cm (1 in) stick cinnamon
3 sections of a star anise
5 cardamoms
4 cups water
1 small can (170 g/6 oz) evaporated milk
2 dessertspoons salt
shallot crisps
hardboiled eggs, sliced

Wash rice and drain well. Wash soaked lentils thoroughly, removing those that float on the surface. Drain in a colander.

Heat oil and ghee in a *kuali* and brown chopped onions and ginger. Put in spices and stir-fry for 1-2 minutes until fragrant. Remove fried ingredients and put into a rice cooker together with water and evaporated milk. Stir to mix and let it come to a boil before adding rice and lentils. Mix well, adding salt. Cook rice for approximately 20 minutes.

Garnish with fried shallot crisps and sliced hard-boiled eggs if desired. Serve hot with Kari Kambing or Ikan, Kurma Ayam or Acar Rampai (pages 6 or 3, 9 or 14 respectively).

Laksa Johor Bersantan

Preparation: 20 minutes Cooking: 30 minutes

Ground Ingredients
40 dried chillies, soaked and seeded
15 shallots
2½ cm (1 in) turmeric root
3 stalks lemon grass
12 slices galingale
1 teaspoon black peppercorns
2½ x 5 cm (1 x 2 in) dried shrimp paste

2 white coconuts, grated (reserve 1 cup for
  'kerisik', add water to remaining grated
  coconut to obtain 12 cups coconut
  milk)
3-4 pieces dried tamarind skin
2 teaspoons salt
½ teaspoon monosodium glutamate
1¼ kg (2¾ lb) wolf herring, steamed
  and flaked
1¼ kg (2¾ lb) fresh thick rice vermicelli,
  scalded and drained
300 g (10 oz) beansprouts
1 cucumber, peeled and shredded
mint leaves

Put ground ingredients into a clay pot together with coconut milk, dried tamarind skin, salt, monosodium glutamate, flaked fish and *kerisik*. Bring to a boil then simmer over low heat for 15 minutes, stirring gravy occasionally.

To serve Laksa, put a little scalded rice vermicelli into individual bowls. Garnish with beansprouts, cucumber and mint leaves. Pour gravy over this and serve hot.

Mee Rebus

Preparation: 40 minutes Cooking: 50 minutes

300 g (10 oz) beef
8 tablespoons oil

Ground Ingredients
20 dried chillies, seeded
30 shallots
4 cloves garlic
5 cm (2 in) turmeric root
2½ cm (1 in) galingale
40 black peppercorns
2 tablespoons preserved soy beans

1 coconut, grated
  (for 12 cups coconut milk)
900 g (2 lb) sweet potatoes,
  steamed   *combined and*
600 g (1⅓ lb) small prawns,   *blended*
  shelled
3 tablespoons rice flour, mixed with a
  little water
1 tablespoon sugar
2 teaspoons salt
600 g (1⅓ lb) fresh yellow
  noodles   *scalded in*
300 g (10 oz) beansprouts,   *boiling water*
  tailed

Garnishing Ingredients
5 hardboiled eggs, quartered
4 stalks spring onion, chopped
5 green chillies, sliced
10 small limes, halved
prawn crisps, crushed lightly

Prawn Crisps
6 tablespoons plain flour, sifted
9 tablespoons water
½ teaspoon salt
½ teaspoon monosodium glutamate
1 tablespoon ground prawns
oil for deep-frying

Cut beef into thin slices.

Heat oil in a *kuali* and fry ground ingredients until fragrant and oil separates. Put in beef and fry for 2 minutes then pour in blended ingredients. Bring to a slow boil, lower heat and simmer for 5-10 minutes. Add rice flour mixed with a little water to thicken gravy, then add sugar and salt. When it comes to a boil again, turn off heat. Reheat again just before serving.

To serve, put some noodles and beansprouts into individual serving bowls. Pour hot gravy over and garnish with hardboiled eggs, spring onions, green chillies, limes and prawn crisps.

Prawn Crisps
Mix flour with water into a smooth batter. Stir in all other ingredients except oil.

Heat oil in a *kuali* until hot. Spoon a tablespoon of batter into hot oil, carefully spreading batter out. Fry over medium heat until golden brown.

Drain on absorbent paper and keep in an airtight container until serving time.

Mee Siam Kering

Preparation: 30 minutes Cooking: 20 minutes

600 g (1 ⅓ lb) rice vermicelli
³/₄ cup oil
20 shallots, sliced
2 firm soybean cakes, cut into small cubes
1 onion, ground
15 dried chillies, soaked ⎫
3 tablespoons dried prawns ⎬ *ground finely*
300 g (10 oz) small prawns, shelled
240 g (8 oz) beef, sliced thinly
2 teaspoons salt
1 teaspoon monosodium glutamate
2 eggs, beaten lightly
3 stalks mustard green, stems
   smashed lightly, cut into 5 cm (2 in)
   lengths (separate stems and leaves)
300 g (10 oz) beansprouts
10-12 stalks Chinese chives,
   cut into 2½ cm (1 in) lengths
3 sprigs Chinese celery, chopped
3 red chillies ⎫
3 green chillies ⎬ *sliced*
10 small limes, halved

Soak vermicelli in water for 10 minutes until soft. Drain in a colander.

Heat oil in a *kuali* and fry sliced shallots until golden brown. Remove with a perforated ladle and leave aside. Fry soybean cakes until lightly browned. Remove and leave aside.

Fry ground onion in the same oil until fragrant, add ground chillies and dried prawns and stir-fry until fragrant. Put in prawns, then add beef, salt and monosodium glutamate.

Pour in beaten eggs and quickly stir-fry. Add mustard green, stems first then leaves. Stir-fry then add fried soybean cakes. Put in rice vermicelli and mix well.

Add beansprouts and Chinese chives and fry briskly for 2 minutes. Lastly, add half the chopped Chinese celery. Place on a large dish and garnish with remaining Chinese celery, red and green chillies and limes and sliced shallot crisps.

Five-spice Meat Roll

Preparation: 30 minutes Cooking: 5 minutes Steaming: 12 minutes

**600 g (1 ⅓ lb) chicken with 2 pieces
   chicken fat or streaky pork, minced**
300 g (10 oz) small prawns, minced
240 g (8 oz) crabmeat
10 cm (4 in) piece carrot
6 water chestnuts } *minced*
5 dried Chinese mushrooms, } *coarsely*
   soaked
2-3 stalks spring onions, chopped

Seasoning Ingredients
½ teaspoon five-spice powder
½ teaspoon salt
½ teaspoon pepper
½ teaspoon monosodium glutamate
½ tablespoon light soy sauce
½ tablespoon sesame oil

½ egg, beaten
1 tablespoon flour
**1 large sheet soybean wrapper, cut into
   30 x 12½ cm (12 x 5 in) pieces**
flour paste
oil for deep-frying
cucumber slices
tomato slices

Combine meat, prawns, crabmeat, carrot, water chestnuts, mushrooms and spring onions and mix with seasoning ingredients, egg and flour. Leave for 1 hour.

Put enough marinated meat mixture in the centre of each soybean wrapper and roll up into 4 cm (1½ in) diameter rolls. Seal edges with a little flour paste.

Place rolls in a steamer and steam for 12 minutes. Cut rolls into 2½ cm (1 in) pieces with a sharp knife.

Heat oil for deep-frying in a *kuali* until hot and fry five-spice rolls until light golden brown.

Serve garnished with cucumber and tomato slices.

Syrup Bandung

(photograph facing page 1)

Preparation: 5 minutes Cooking: 5 minutes Makes: 4 cups

2 cups water
120 g (4 oz) sugar
3 screwpine leaves, knotted
1 small can (170 g/6 oz) evaporated milk
pinch of salt
2-3 drops red colouring
1 large bottle ice cream soda

Put water, sugar and screwpine leaves in a saucepan and boil until sugar dissolves. Cool. Discard screwpine leaves.

Combine cooled syrup with evaporated milk, salt, colouring and lastly ice cream soda. Mix well and serve thoroughly chilled.

Note: Syrup Bandung is popularly served as a refreshing drink at Malay wedding feasts.

Kuih Koleh-koleh Kacang

(photograph facing page 1)

Preparation: 15 minutes Cooking: 1 hour 10 minutes

Topping/Tahi Minyak
1 coconut, grated (for 1 cup 'pati santan')

Kuih
300 g (10 oz) green beans, soaked for at least 2 hours, preferably overnight
4 cups water
1½ coconuts, grated (for 3 cups thick coconut milk)
450 g (1 lb) palm sugar, cut into small pieces
½ cup water
2 screwpine leaves

Note: Green bean flour, if available, can be used instead. Simply sift flour and stir in coconut milk without adding water. If Kuih Koleh-koleh turns out to be your favourite, as it is mine, then it is worth the effort to wash as much as 2-3 kilograms of beans, during your spare time of course, pan fry or oven toast until dry, then send to the mill for grinding. It keeps well for months especially in the refrigerator.

To wash green beans and thoroughly remove small stones and grit, wash and scoop beans with fingers into a separate container instead of draining water away from pan. This way the heavier sand and grit will remain at the bottom of the pan. Do this several times.

Coconut residue crisps when drained from oil and cooled can be stored in an airtight container for as long as a week without refrigeration. A tablespoon or two of this added to Sambal Prawns with slightly thicker gravy imparts a delightful flavour.

Topping
Put *pati santan* into a *kuali* and stir over low heat with a wooden spatula for 30-35 minutes. Oil will separate from coconut residue. Continue stirring until coconut residue turns a rich brown. Remove from heat and drain.

Kuih
Wash green beans and put in a pressure cooker with 4 cups water. Pressure cook for 20 minutes. Put in a blender with coconut milk and blend until fine. For easier and finer blending, do this a third at a time. If blender is not turning well, add a little extra coconut milk.

Melt palm sugar with water over heat, stirring frequently. Strain into blended mixture. Mix well.

Pour mixture into a *kuali,* add screwpine leaves and stir continuously with a wooden spatula over low heat for 15 minutes or until it becomes a thick paste. Do not allow mixture to stick to bottom of *kuali.* When paste is thick enough make a figure '8' with the spatula. If it holds well, paste is of right consistency. Discard screwpine leaves.

Spoon into an 18 x 27 cm (7 x 11 in) shallow tin and smooth surface whilst hot with a piece of banana leaf or a butter knife. Sprinkle with prepared coconut residue crisps. Leave to cool thoroughly before cutting.

Kuih Bakar Jagung

Preparation: 15 minutes   Baking: 50 minutes   Makes: 21

1 can (450 g/1 lb) sweetcorn
1½ coconuts, grated (for 2⅔ cups
    coconut milk)
240 g (8 oz) flour
195 g (6½ oz) granulated sugar
4 eggs, beaten lightly with a fork
1 tablespoon margarine, melted
1 teaspoon vanilla essence

Note: If Kuih Bakar patty tins are not available, use the normal cupcake patty tins which are slightly shallower.

Put sweetcorn and a little of the coconut milk in a blender and blend until fine. Leave aside.

Sift flour into a mixing bowl, add sugar and stir in remaining coconut milk a little at a time until smooth. If batter is lumpy, put through a strainer.

Stir in eggs, blended sweetcorn, melted margarine and vanilla essence.

Grease individual Kuih Bakar patty tins with margarine. Fill patty tins with sweetcorn batter and bake in a moderate oven for 50 minutes until top is lightly browned.

Allow to cool before turning out. Loosen *kuih* by running a round-bladed knife along edge of patty tin. Kuih Bakar will sink slightly in the centre as it cools.

Kuih Nagasari

Preparation: 30 minutes   Cooking: 30 minutes   Makes: 16

240 g (8 oz) rice flour
2 cups water
1 coconut, grated (for 3½ cups coconut
    milk)
2 screwpine leaves, knotted
½ teaspoon salt
16 banana leaves, cut into 18 x 15 cm
    (7 x 6 in) pieces, scalded
8 small ripe bananas ('pisang rajah'),
    peeled and halved lengthwise

Sift rice flour into a bowl, add water and blend mixture until smooth. Place coconut milk, screwpine leaves and salt in a saucepan and bring to a slow boil. Add rice batter to coconut milk and stir with a wooden spoon for approximately 5 minutes until mixture turns into a smooth paste. Remove from heat.

Place a dessertspoonful of cooked mixture in the centre of each banana leaf. Fold one side of banana leaf to flatten mixture into a small rectangle. Top with a piece of banana and cover with another spoonful of dough mixture. Fold banana leaf, overlapping lengthwise to cover mixture and tuck the other ends under. Steam for 20 minutes and serve hot or cold.

MALACCA

Steeped in history, Malacca is Malaysia's oldest and historically most important city, though not much of its history before the fourteenth century is known. Founded by a Malay noble in that century, it flourished and attracted traders from near and far for spices, silks, ivory and gold. Admiral Cheng Ho forged the first link with Malacca and eventually Chinese settled there. At the turn of the century, Malacca fell to the Portuguese who were to remain for some 130 years, making the port one of the mightiest fortresses in the east. Malacca then fell to the Dutch and they held the city for more than a century and a half.

The distinct legacy of this historic and picturesque past is inherited in the wide variety of food one is fortunate to savour in Malacca, very often an exciting and rich potpourri of Malay, Nonya and Portuguese foods.

Malay food is deliciously hot and sour — like Ikan Masak Kuah Lada, Daging Masak Asam Tumis and Ikan Masak Lemak. Nonya food, a blend of Chinese and Malay cuisines, is cooked Malay style with lots of coconut milk, spices, chillies and fragrant roots and grasses. However, Chinese ingredients such as pork, dried Chinese mushrooms and soy sauce are used, giving the typically Nonya Ayam or Babi Pong Tay, Ayam Tempra and Ayam Sioh. Portuguese-influenced dishes are sour and spicy with generous use of tamarind as well as vinegar. Dishes like Feng, Pada, Debal Chicken and Vindaloo are popular within the community, and though not as well known as other cuisines, are tantalisingly delicious.

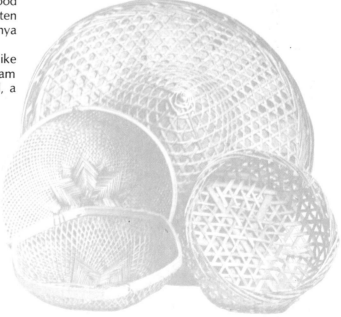

Opposite: Popiah

Ikan Masak Kuah Lada

Preparation: 15 minutes   Cooking: 20 minutes

450 g (1 lb) wolf herring, cut into
    9 cm (3½ in) slices
1 teaspoon salt
4 tablespoons oil

Ground Ingredients
10 red chillies, seeded
8 shallots
3 cloves garlic
2 tablespoons coriander
1 teaspoon fennel
1 teaspoon black peppercorns
1 teaspoon turmeric powder

4 tablespoons white grated coconut for
    'kerisik', ground separately
1 dessertspoon tamarind paste ⎫ *mixed and*
1½ cups water   ⎬ *strained*
1 teaspoon salt
½ teaspoon monosodium glutamate

Rub fish with salt and leave for 15 minutes.

Heat oil in a *kuali* and fry ground ingredients until fragrant. Add *kerisik* and fry for 2 minutes over low heat. Pour in tamarind juice. When it comes to a boil, add fish and cook for 8-10 minutes until fish is done. Stir in salt and monosodium glutamate.

Ikan Masak Lemak

Preparation: 10 minutes   Grilling: 25-30 minutes· Cooking: 12 minutes

2 horse mackerels
1 teaspoon salt

Ground Ingredients
12 dried chillies, soaked
8 shallots
1 teaspoon turmeric powder

1 coconut, grated (for 2 cups coconut
    milk)
2 small pieces dried tamarind skin
180 g (6 oz) salted Tientsin cabbage,
    sliced
½ teaspoon salt
½ teaspoon monosodium glutamate

Wash fish but do not remove the hard skin. Rub with salt and grill each side for 15 minutes until just cooked. Gently remove the hard skin.

Put ground ingredients, coconut milk and tamarind skin into an earthen pot and bring to a slow boil. Add salted Tientsin cabbage and simmer for 10 minutes over low heat.

Add fish, salt and monosodium glutamate. Cook for 2 minutes and remove from heat.

Ikan Garam Asam

Preparation: 15 minutes   Cooking: 15 minutes

600 g (1 ⅓ lb) black pomfret or
  spanish mackerel
1 teaspoon salt
6 tablespoons oil

Ground Ingredients
12 red chillies
10 dried chillies, soaked
1 stalk lemon grass
2½ cm (1 in) galingale
2½ cm (1 in) turmeric root
1¼ cm (½ in) square dried shrimp paste
8 candlenuts

6 small sour starfruit, halved lengthwise
3 tablespoons tamarind paste | *mixed and*
2 cups water | *strained*
1 dessertspoon sugar
1 teaspoon salt

Season fish with salt and leave for 15 minutes.

Heat oil in an earthen pot and fry ground ingredients until fragrant. Put in small sour starfruit and stir-fry for a minute then add tamarind juice, a little at a time, whilst frying. Bring to a boil, then lower heat and simmer for 5 minutes.

Add sugar, salt and fish and cook until fish is done.

Ikan Bawal Masak Kuah Lada

Preparation: 15 minutes   Cooking: 20 minutes

1 medium black pomfret,
  cut into 4-5 pieces
1 teaspoon salt
4 tablespoons oil
2 stalks lemon grass, crushed lightly

Ground Ingredients
30 g (1 oz) white peppercorns
5 candlenuts
6 shallots
4 cloves garlic | *ground coarsely*
1¼ x 2½ cm (½ x 1 in) dried shrimp paste
1¼ cm (½ in) turmeric root

180 g (6 oz) salted Tientsin cabbage,
  sliced
2 heaped dessertspoons tamarind paste | *mixed and*
4 cups water | *strained*
1 teaspoon salt

Rub fish with salt and leave for 15 minutes.

Heat oil in an earthen pot and fry lemon grass for 2 minutes. Add ground ingredients and fry until fragrant.

Put in salted Tientsin cabbage and stir-fry for 1-2 minutes. Pour in tamarind juice and bring to a slow boil. Add fish and salt and remove from heat when fish is cooked.

Pada (Saltfish Pickle)

(photograph opposite)

Preparation: 15 minutes   Cooking: 40 minutes

600 g (1⅓ lb) saltfish (threadfin)
1½ cups oil

Ground Ingredients
15 shallots
4 whole pods garlic
7½ cm (3 in) ginger
5 tablespoons vindaloo curry
    powder (page 37) ⎫ *mixed*
5 tablespoons water ⎭

2 cups vinegar
3 tablespoons tamarind paste ⎫ *mixed and*
¼ cup water ⎭ *strained*
240 g (8 oz) sugar ⎫ *boiled to*
¼ cup water ⎭ *dissolve sugar*

Wash saltfish, then cut into 2 cm (¾ in) square pieces and dry in the sun for 2 hours.

Heat oil in a *kuali* and deep-fry saltfish over low heat for 7-10 minutes until golden brown and crisp. Drain from oil.

Strain oil from *kuali* into an earthen pot. When hot, fry ground ingredients over low heat until fragrant. Add vinegar, tamarind juice and syrup and bring to a slow boil. Simmer for 12-15 minutes until gravy is thick and a thick layer of oil appears on surface.

Cool gravy thoroughly before putting in fried saltfish. Store in small airtight jars.

Note: Saltfish Pickle keeps well for as long as a year in the refrigerator. It goes well with rice and is delicious as a sandwich spread.

Instead of saltfish, fresh fish, preferably spanish mackerel (ikan tenggiri), can be used. Deep-fry fish slices until cooked then pour prepared gravy over fish.

Fried Tamarind Prawns

Preparation: 5 minutes   Cooking: 5 minutes

600 g (1⅓ lb) large prawns
2 heaped tablespoons tamarind paste ⎫ *mixed and*
4 tablespoons water ⎭ *strained*
1 teaspoon salt
½ teaspoon pepper
½ teaspoon sugar
½ teaspoon monosodium glutamate
1 cup oil
1 cucumber, sliced

Trim off eye portion and legs of prawns. Keep shells intact.

Marinate prawns with thick tamarind juice, salt, pepper, sugar and monosodium glutamate and leave for 15 minutes.

Heat oil in a *kuali* until hot and fry prawns over moderate heat for 3-5 minutes until prawns are cooked. Place on a dish garnished with cucumber.

Sambal Udang Kering

Preparation: 15 minutes   Cooking: 30 minutes

300 g (10 oz) dried prawns
5 tablespoons oil

Ground Ingredients
35 dried chillies, soaked
240 g (8 oz) shallots
6 stalks lemon grass, sliced
1¼ cm (½ in) turmeric root

2 tablespoons tamarind paste } *mixed and*
¼ cup water   } *strained*
1 teaspoon sugar
½ teaspoon monosodium glutamate
8 shallots, sliced and fried crisp

Soak dried prawns in water for half an hour. Rinse, drain and squeeze dry. Blend in an electric chopper or pound prawns finely.

Heat oil in a *kuali* until hot then fry ground ingredients for a few minutes over low heat until fragrant.

Add ground prawns then thick tamarind juice, sugar and monosodium glutamate. Stir-fry continuously until dry. Remove and when cool mix with shallot crisps.

Store in airtight jars.

Note: Sambal Udang Kering keeps well in the refrigerator. It is delicious with toasted bread or as a sandwich spread.

Cuttlefish in Tamarind

Preparation: 15 minutes Cooking: 20 minutes

450 g (1 lb) small-medium cuttlefish
3 tablespoons tamarind paste } *mixed and*
2½ cups water   } *strained*
1¼ cm (½ in) square dried shrimp paste
1 dessertspoon sugar
1 teaspoon salt
3 pieces dried tamarind skin
12 shallots, sliced
2 stalks lemon grass, crushed
4 red chillies   } *stems retained,*
4 green chillies } *split lengthwise*

Wash and remove ink sac from cuttlefish.

Put tamarind juice, dried shrimp paste, sugar, salt, tamarind skin, shallots and lemon grass into a pot. Bring to a boil then add red and green chillies.

Simmer gently for 10 minutes. Add cuttlefish and boil for 3-4 minutes until just cooked.

Rendang Daging Lembu

Preparation: 20 minutes   Cooking: 1½ hours

600 g (1⅓ lb) beef, cut into 6 mm (¼ in) thick slices

Ground Ingredients
15 dried chillies, soaked
3 tablespoons coriander
1 teaspoon fennel
1 teaspoon black peppercorns
4 stalks lemon grass
12 shallots
4 cm (1½ in) galingale
4 cm (1½ in) ginger

1½ coconuts, grated (for 5 cups coconut milk)
½ white coconut, grated for 'kerisik'
2 turmeric leaves
1½ teaspoons salt
½ teaspoon monosodium glutamate

Cut beef into slices and drain in a colander.

Put beef, ground ingredients and coconut milk in an earthen pot and bring to a slow boil.

Simmer gently for 1¼ hours, stirring frequently, until gravy is thick. Add *kerisik,* turmeric leaves, salt and monosodium glutamate and continue stirring until gravy is almost dry and meat is tender.

Daging Masak Asam Tumis

Preparation: 20 minutes   Cooking: 45 minutes

600 g (1⅓ lb) beef, cut into 6 mm (¼ in) thick slices
5 tablespoons oil

Ground Ingredients
30 dried chillies, soaked
15 shallots
3 cloves garlic
2½ cm (1 in) turmeric root

2 stalks lemon grass, crushed lightly
4 cm (1½ in) galingale, crushed lightly
2 heaped dessertspoons tamarind paste | *mixed and*
2 cups water | *strained*
½ teaspoon monosodium glutamate
1½ teaspoons salt

Cut meat into slices and drain in a colander.

Heat oil in an earthen pot and fry ground ingredients until fragrant and oil separates. Put in meat and stir-fry for a few minutes.

Add crushed lemon grass, galingale and tamarind juice. Bring to a boil and simmer gently for 30 minutes until meat is tender and gravy thick. Stir in monosodium glutamate and salt to taste.

Feng (Curry Mixture of Meats)

Preparation: 1 hour   Cooking: 45 minutes

300 g (10 oz) cow's or pig's intestine
2 teaspoons salt
a little vinegar
300 g (10 oz) lung, halved lengthwise
2 teaspoons salt
a little vinegar
300 g (10 oz) beef or pork
300 g (10 oz) heart
300 g (10 oz) liver
1 cup oil
5 cm (2 in) ginger, cut into strips

Ground Ingredients

2 tablespoons coriander
1 dessertspoon fennel
1 dessertspoon cummin
1 tablespoon white peppercorns
2½ cm (1 in) dried turmeric root or
   1 teaspoon turmeric powder
6 candlenuts
10 shallots
5 cloves garlic

2 cups stock
3 teaspoons salt
2 tablespoons vinegar

Turn intestine inside out with a chopstick, rub with salt and vinegar and wash thoroughly. Rub lung with salt and vinegar and wash thoroughly. Place intestine and lung in a pressure cooker with some water and cook for 30 minutes until tender. Drain and when cool cut into 6 mm (¼ in) cubes. Discard water in the pressure cooker.

Boil a saucepan of water, put in beef or pork and heart and cook for 15 minutes. Remove and drain.

Put in liver and cook for 5 minutes until just cooked. Remove and drain. When cool, cut beef or pork, heart and liver into 6 mm (¼ in) cubes. Retain 2 cups of the meat stock for cooking.

Heat oil in a *kuali* and lightly brown ginger strips. Drain from oil and leave aside.

Add ground ingredients to oil and fry over low heat until fragrant. Put in all diced ingredients except liver and stir well.

Add stock and bring to a slow boil. Lower heat and simmer until meat is tender and very little gravy remains. Add liver, ginger, salt and vinegar.

Note: Feng is a traditional Portuguese Eurasian dish served for Christmas.

Beef Semur (Stew)

Preparation: 15 minutes   Cooking: 1¼ hours

600 g (1⅓ lb) beef, cut into 2½ x 2½ x
    5 cm (1 x 1 x 2 in) chunks
1 dessertspoon pepper
2 tablespoons light soy sauce
1 teaspoon dark soy sauce
2 tablespoons vinegar
3 tablespoons oil
2 large onions, sliced
4 cloves
¼ piece nutmeg
2½ cm (1 in) stick cinnamon
6 cups hot water
4 potatoes, skinned and kept whole
1 teaspoon salt

Marinate beef with pepper, light soy sauce, dark soy sauce and vinegar and leave for 30 minutes.

Heat oil in a pot or *kuali* and fry onions until transparent. Put in spices and fry until fragrant. Add beef and stir for a few minutes.

Pour in water and bring to a boil. Lower heat and simmer, covered, for 1 hour, stirring occasionally. Halfway through cooking add potatoes and salt.

Semur (Oxtail Stew)

Preparation: 15 minutes   Cooking: 50 minutes

1 kg (2⅕ lb) ox tail, cut into 4 cm
    (1½ in) pieces
9 cups water
2 tablespoons oil
2 onions, sliced

Ground Ingredients
2½ cm (1 in) stick cinnamon
5 cloves
¼ piece nutmeg

1 tablespoon light soy sauce
1 teaspoon dark soy sauce
4 medium potatoes, halved
1½ teaspoons salt
1 teaspoon vinegar

Put ox tail and water into a pressure cooker and cook for 30 minutes.

Heat oil in a cooking pot or *kuali* and fry onions until transparent. Add spices and fry until fragrant.

Pour in ox tail together with stock. Bring to a boil. Add light soy sauce, dark soy sauce and potatoes. Simmer over low heat until potatoes are cooked, then add salt and vinegar.

Ayam Tempra

Preparation: 15 minutes   Cooking: 25 minutes

1 kg (2¹/₅ lb) chicken, cut into bite-size
  pieces
1 teaspoon salt
5 tablespoons oil
15 shallots ⎫
3 onions ⎬ *sliced*
4 red chillies ⎭

Sauce
1 cup water
2 tablespoons dark soy sauce
1 tablespoon sugar
1 teaspoon salt
¼ teaspoon monosodium glutamate

Season chicken with salt and leave aside.

Heat oil in a *kuali* and fry sliced ingredients until fragrant and transparent. Put in chicken and stir-fry over high heat for 5-7 minutes until chicken is lightly browned.

Add sauce ingredients and bring to a boil. Cover *kuali* and simmer for 15-20 minutes until chicken is tender and sauce is thick.

Chicken Debal Curry

(photograph opposite)

Preparation: 20 minutes   Cooking: 25 minutes

1½ kg (3⅓ lb) chicken, cut into bite-size
  pieces
1 teaspoon salt
8 tablespoons oil
6 shallots ⎫
3 cloves garlic ⎬ *sliced*
3 red chillies ⎭

Ground Ingredients
30 dried chillies, soaked
5 red chillies
5 cm (2 in) ginger
15 shallots
3 cloves garlic
8 candlenuts
1 tablespoon coriander
1 teaspoon turmeric powder

1 tablespoon mustard seeds, crushed
  lightly
1½ cups water
1½ tablespoons rice vinegar ⎫
1 dessertspoon dark soy sauce ⎬ *combined*
2 teaspoons mustard ⎭
1 teaspoon salt

Season chicken with salt and leave aside.

Heat oil in a *kuali* and lightly brown sliced ingredients. Put in ground ingredients and fry for 5 minutes then add mustard seeds and fry until fragrant.

Put in chicken and fry for a few minutes then add water and bring to a boil. Lower heat and simmer, covered, for 15 minutes, stirring occasionally until chicken is tender. Add combined rice vinegar, dark soy sauce and mustard and salt. Stir well and remove from heat.

Note: Debal or Devil Curry as it is more popularly known means hot curry.

Opposite: Chicken Debal Curry

Devil

Preparation: 20 minutes   Cooking: 25 minutes

1½ kg (3⅓ lb) chicken, cut into bite-size
  pieces
1 teaspoon salt
8 tablespoons oil
2 onions, sliced

Ground Ingredients
10 dried chillies, soaked
6 red chillies
12 shallots
5 cloves garlic
2½ cm (1 in) ginger
2½ cm (1 in) turmeric root
8 candlenuts

1 tablespoon mustard seeds ⎤
6 tablespoons rice vinegar ⎦ combined
1¼ cups water
3 potatoes, quartered
1 teaspoon salt

Season chicken with salt and leave aside.

Heat oil in a *kuali* and lightly brown onions. Put in ground ingredients and fry for 5 minutes, then add mustard seeds and vinegar. Bring to a slow boil then put in chicken and fry for a few minutes.

Add water and when it comes to a boil, lower heat, add potatoes and simmer till chicken is tender and potatoes cooked. Add salt to taste.

Note: This version of Devil is delicious, using leftover roast chicken or roast pork. Add 1 tablespoon coriander to ground ingredients and ½ cup water or gravy from meat if available.

Ayam/Babi Pong Tay (Stewed Chicken or Pork)

Preparation: 15 minutes   Cooking: 40 minutes

1 kg (2⅕ lb) chicken, or 600 g (1⅓ lb)
  streaky pork
½ teaspoon salt
6 tablespoons oil
180 g (6 oz) shallots ⎤
3 whole pods garlic ⎦ ground
2 tablespoons preserved soy beans
4-5 dried Chinese mushrooms, soaked
2 cups water
1 teaspoon dark soy sauce
3 potatoes, quartered
½ teaspoon salt

Cut chicken into small pieces and if using pork cut into 5 x 2½ cm (2 x 1 in) pieces. Season meat with salt and leave aside.

Heat oil in a *kuali* and fry ground shallots and garlic for 2 minutes, then add preserved soy beans and fry over low heat until fragrant.

Put in mushrooms, then meat and stir-fry for a few minutes. Add water and dark soy sauce and bring to a boil. Lower heat and simmer, covered, for 15 minutes, then add potatoes and salt. Simmer gently for a further 12-15 minutes until meat is tender and sauce is quite thick.

Chicken Vindaloo

Preparation: 15 minutes   Cooking: 30 minutes

1 kg (2¹/₅ lb) chicken, pork or beef
8 tablespoons oil

Ground Ingredients
15 shallots
10 cloves garlic
2½ cm (1 in) ginger

3 tablespoons vindaloo curry powder
   (below), mixed to a paste with a
   little water
½ cup vinegar
1 cup water
1½ teaspoons salt

Cut chicken into small pieces. If using pork or beef, cut into 6 mm (¼ in) thick slices.

Heat oil in a pan and fry ground ingredients for a minute, then add curry paste and fry until fragrant and oil separates.

Add vinegar, a little at a time, while frying ground ingredients. Put in meat and fry for a few minutes over high heat. Add water and salt and simmer over low heat for 15 minutes until chicken is tender and gravy thick.

Note: Vindaloo is a Portuguese Indian dish from Kerala. If prepared vindaloo curry powder is not available, use 20 dried chillies, soaked, 1½ tablespoons cummin and 2 teaspoons mustard seeds ground to a paste together with shallots, garlic and ginger.

Vindaloo Curry Powder

Preparation: 20 minutes

600 g (1⅓ lb) dried chillies, stems removed
600 g (1⅓ lb) cummin
300 g (10 oz) mustard seeds

Wash each ingredient separately and dry in the sun for 2-3 days in large flat trays or bamboo baskets, turning spices occasionally to make sure ingredients are thoroughly dried.

When well dried, send spices to the mill to be ground to a fine powder. Spread out and cool before storing in airtight containers.

The curry powder will keep for a few months.

Note: Use vindaloo curry powder for Chicken, Beef or Pork Vindaloo and Pada — Salted Fish or Fresh Fish Pickle.

Ayam Goreng Rempah

Preparation: 15 minutes   Cooking: 30 minutes

1½ kg (3⅓ lb) chicken, cut into bite-size
    pieces
1 teaspoon turmeric powder
1 teaspoon salt
oil for deep-frying

Ground Ingredients
10 red chillies
10 shallots
5 cloves garlic
4 cm (1½ in) ginger
3 stalks lemon grass
3 tablespoons coriander
1 teaspoon fennel
1 teaspoon black peppercorns

1 turmeric leaf
1 teaspoon salt
½ teaspoon monosodium glutamate

Marinate chicken with turmeric powder and salt and leave for 30 minutes.

Heat oil in a *kuali* and deep-fry chicken for 15 minutes till golden brown. Remove and drain.

Leave 4 tablespoons oil in the *kuali* and fry ground ingredients until fragrant and oil separates.

Add turmeric leaf and put in fried chicken. Stir-fry over low heat until chicken is cooked and well coated with ground ingredients. Add salt and monosodium glutamate before removing from heat.

Ayam Sioh (Tamarind Chicken)

Preparation: 15 minutes   Cooking: 40 minutes

1 chicken (1½ kg/3⅓ lb), cut into 8 large
    pieces

Tamarind Sauce
360 g (12 oz) tamarind paste ⎫ *mixed and*
3¼ cups water ⎭ *strained*
1½ tablespoons rice vinegar
2 tablespoons dark soy sauce
10 tablespoons sugar
2 teaspoons salt
3 tablespoons roasted coriander powder
12 shallots
3 cloves garlic ⎭ *ground*

6 tablespoons oil

Marinate chicken with tamarind sauce in a large bowl and leave overnight in the refrigerator.

Next day, pour tamarind sauce into a pot and bring to a slow boil. Add chicken pieces and boil over moderate heat for 20 minutes or until chicken is tender.

Drain chicken in a colander and continue cooking sauce, stirring frequently until thick. Remove from heat.

Heat 6 tablespoons oil in a *kuali* until hot and fry chicken for a few minutes until brown. Arrange on a dish and pour thick tamarind sauce over chicken.

Serve hot or cold.

Portuguese Acar

Preparation: 40 minutes   Cooking: 20 minutes

450 g (1 lb) green chillies, stems retained
1 tablespoon lime paste
1 cucumber, quartered lengthwise, soft
  portions removed, cut into 4 cm (1½ in)
  pieces
2 teaspoons salt
240 g (8 oz) cauliflower, cut into small
  pieces
2 teaspoons salt
1 cup sugar ⎫
½ cup water ⎬ *combined*
2 tablespoons mustard seeds, washed and
  dried in the sun
½ cup oil
7½ cm (3 in) turmeric root ⎫
120 g (4 oz) dried prawns, ⎬ *ground*
  washed and drained ⎭
6 cups vinegar
10 cloves garlic, sliced and fried crisp

Wash green chillies in a basin of water mixed with lime paste. Drain and wash thoroughly with water, then dry chillies with a clean cloth.

Make a 5 cm (2 in) slit from the stem end to the centre of each chilli and if desired remove seeds.

Rub cucumber with salt and lightly squeeze cucumber to remove juice, then dry in the sun for 2 hours.

Sprinkle cauliflower with salt and leave aside.

Put combined sugar and water in a small saucepan and bring to a slow boil to dissolve sugar. Leave syrup aside.

Lightly crush mustard seeds and remove the outer skins. Put aside.

Heat oil in a pan and fry ground ingredients until fragrant. Add vinegar and bring to a slow boil. Put in syrup and stir until it boils again. Remove from heat and pour into a deep bowl. Allow vinegar mixture to cool completely. Put in mustard seeds, prepared green chillies, cucumber, cauliflower and garlic crisps. Stir well and leave for 3 days before serving.

Kacang Panjang Masak Lemak Udang

Preparation: 15 minutes   Cooking: 20 minutes

360 g (12 oz) long beans, cut into 5 cm
    (2 in) lengths
300 g (10 oz) small prawns, shelled
½ teaspoon salt
6 tablespoons oil

Ground Ingredients
5 red chillies
6 shallots
3 candlenuts
1¼ cm (½ in) cube dried shrimp paste

60 g (2 oz) dried prawns, soaked and
    ground coarsely
1 coconut, grated (for 1 cup thick coconut
    milk and 2 cups thin coconut milk)

Cut long beans into 5 cm (2 in) lengths. Season prawns with salt and leave for 15 minutes.

Heat oil in a *kuali* and fry ground ingredients for a few minutes then add dried prawns and fry until fragrant.

Put in long beans and stir-fry for a minute. Add thin coconut milk and bring to a boil. Simmer for 5 minutes or until beans are just tender but not too soft. Add prawns, cook for a minute then pour in thick coconut milk. When gravy boils, remove from heat.

Laksa Lemak Melaka

(photograph opposite)

Preparation: 25 minutes   Cooking: 25 minutes

1¼ cups oil

Ground Ingredients
600 g (1⅓ lb) shallots
5 cm (2 in) turmeric root
40 dried chillies, soaked
6 red chillies
4 x 5 cm (1½ x 2 in) dried shrimp paste
10 candlenuts
6 stalks lemon grass
2½ x 5 cm (1 x 2 in) galingale
60 g (2 oz) dried prawns

1 kg (2¹/₅ lb) large prawns, shells retained
3 coconuts, grated (for 16 cups
    coconut milk)
3 fish cakes, sliced
3 teaspoons salt
1 teaspoon monosodium glutamate
1½ kg (3⅓ lb) fresh thick rice
    vermicelli, or 2 packets dried thick
    rice vermicelli, scalded and drained

Garnishing Ingredients
600 g (1⅓ lb) beansprouts, tailed and
    scalded
2 cucumbers, peeled and shredded
2 bunches mint leaves

Heat oil in a *kuali* and fry ground ingredients until fragrant and oil appears on surface. Put in large prawns and stir-fry for 3 minutes until prawns are cooked. Dish out the prawns only and leave aside. This will prevent prawns from being overcooked.

Pour in coconut milk and bring to a boil. Put in fish cake slices. When gravy boils again put in prawns, salt and monosodium glutamate.

To serve, put a little thick rice vermicelli into individual serving bowls. Garnish with beansprouts, cucumber and mint leaves. Pour hot gravy with prawns and fish slices over this.

Opposite: Laksa Lemak Melaka

Popiah

(photograph on page 24)

Preparation: (filling and garnishing) 2 hours (egg skins) 1¼ hours   Makes: approximately 48-50 medium Popiahs

Filling
600 g (1⅓ lb) chicken meat or belly pork,
   cut into thin strips
1 teaspoon salt
600 g (1⅓ lb) small prawns, shelled
   (shells reserved for stock)
1 teaspoon salt
9 cups water
7 tablespoons oil
3 whole pods garlic, minced
5 tablespoons preserved soy beans,
   ground lightly
2 kg (4½ lb) turnip, shredded
3 cans (552 g/1 lb 3½ oz each) bamboo
   shoots, drained and shredded
10 firm soybean cakes, cut into strips
   and fried
1 teaspoon salt

Garnishing Ingredients
2 heads lettuce
20 red chillies, ground
3 whole pods garlic, ground
black sweet sauce
600 g (1⅓ lb) beansprouts, tailed and
   scalded
1 large cucumber, shredded finely
300 g (10 oz) small prawns, shelled
   and steamed
5 eggs   *made into thin*
¼ teaspoon salt   *omelettes and*
¼ teaspoon pepper   *sliced finely*
4 medium crabs, steamed and
   meat extracted
300 g (10 oz) roasted peanuts, ground
300 g (10 oz) shallots, sliced and
   fried crisp

Egg Skin
10 eggs
8½ cups water
600 g (1⅓ lb) flour
½ teaspoon salt

Note: To make smooth egg skins, pan has to be just hot to set skin. If it is too hot skin will turn out perforated.

Filling
Season meat with salt and leave aside. Season prawns with salt and leave aside.

Boil prawn shells in water for 5-10 minutes. Strain.

Heat oil in a *kuali* and lightly brown garlic. Add preserved soy beans and fry until fragrant. Pour in prawn stock and when it comes to a boil add turnip and bamboo shoots. When it starts to boil again add meat. Simmer gently for 1½ hours or transfer to a pressure cooker and pressure cook for 30 minutes. Add soybean cakes, prawns and salt to taste and simmer for another 10 minutes.

This filling may be prepared a day early, kept refrigerated and reheated before use.

Garnishing Ingredients
Prepare garnishing ingredients while cooking filling. To cut preparation time, crabmeat can be extracted a day ahead and frozen. Roasted ground peanuts and shallot crisps can also be prepared well ahead and kept in airtight containers.

Egg Skin
Lightly beat eggs with a fork and gradually stir in water. Sift flour into a bowl and add egg mixture gradually together with salt. Blend well and strain mixture to remove lumps. Leave for 20 minutes.

Lightly grease a 25 cm (10 in) non-stick pan with a brush. Heat. Pour a ladleful of batter (about 3 tablespoons) or enough to spread over base of pan thinly, and cook over very low heat for 2 minutes or until pancake leaves side of pan. Remove and place on a flat dish. Repeat process and stack egg skins until batter is used up.

To serve Popiah, put an egg skin on a plate. Place a piece of lettuce on the edge. Spread with as much fresh ground chilli, ground garlic, black sweet sauce, beansprouts and cucumber as desired. Place 2 tablespoons of filling, drained of gravy, on top, then add a few steamed prawns, omelette strips and crabmeat. Sprinkle a little roasted ground peanuts and shallot crisps on top. Wrap and carefully roll up like a swiss roll.

Kuih Buah Melaka

Preparation: 20 minutes   Cooking: 10 minutes   Makes: 38-40

240 g (8 oz) glutinous rice flour
¾ cup boiling hot water
1 tablespoon screwpine juice ⎫ combined
a few drops green colouring ⎭
120 g (4 oz) palm sugar, cut into
    small pieces
½ white grated coconut ⎫ mixed
pinch of salt ⎭

*Note: Kuih Buah Melaka is also commonly
known as Kuih Onde Onde. To obtain screwpine juice, pound 5-6 screwpine leaves with
a little water or blend in a blender. Press out
juice and strain.*

Sift glutinous rice flour into a bowl. Add combined
boiling hot water, screwpine juice and green
colouring, mix well and knead into a firm lump of
dough.

Form into marble-size balls. Flatten each ball
lightly and fill with 1 or 2 pieces of palm sugar.
Press edges together and shape into small balls.

Boil half a saucepan of water, put in the glutinous
rice balls, a few at a time. When cooked, glutinous rice balls will rise to the surface. Dish out
with a perforated ladle and roll them in grated
coconut mixed with salt.

Pengat

Preparation: 10 minutes   Cooking: 50 minutes   Serves: 6

700 g (1½ lb) yam
1 coconut, grated (for 1 cup thick
    coconut milk and 3 cups thin
    coconut milk)
180 g (6 oz) palm sugar, chopped
90 g (3 oz) sugar
4 screwpine leaves, knotted
4 medium bananas ('pisang rajah')

Peel yam and cut into 3 portions. Steam over
rapidly boiling water for 25 minutes. When cool,
cut into 2½ x 5 cm (1 x 2 in) thick pieces.

Put thin coconut milk, palm sugar, sugar and
screwpine leaves in a saucepan, simmer and stir
gently for 5 minutes to melt sugar. Add steamed
yam and simmer gently for 15 minutes.

Peel and cut bananas at a slant into thick slices.
Put into coconut milk mixture. When mixture
boils, add thick coconut milk.

Serve hot or cold for tea or as a sweet.

Bolu Koku (Coconut Sponge Cake)

Preparation: 20 minutes   Baking: 50 minutes   Oven setting: 175°C, 350°F, Gas Regulo 6

6 large eggs
300 g (10 oz) castor sugar
1 teaspoon vanilla essence
240 g (8 oz) flour ⎫ sifted
¼ teaspoon cinnamon powder ⎭ together
240 g (8 oz) white grated coconut,
    ground finely
pinch of salt

Whisk eggs, sugar and vanilla essence until light
and fluffy. Gradually add sifted flour and cinnamon to egg mixture. Stir in ground coconut and
salt.

Pour batter into a greased 22 cm (9 in) tube pan
and bake in a moderate oven for 50 minutes until
top is golden brown.

NEGRI SEMBILAN

The name Negri Sembilan, literally 'nine states', alludes to the loose federation ruled by Malay chiefs before they were united under the British administration. Seremban, the state capital, with its narrow streets and backlanes, is typical of many of the towns that grew from the tin-mining centres many years ago. Travelling through, one cannot help noticing the distinctive Minangkabau (buffalo horns) influence, strongly reflected in the style of houses with roofs that sweep to two horn-like peaks.

Malay food is similarly Minangkabau influenced. Most of their offerings are burning hot with a generous use of bird chillies to give an extra kick. Well-prepared Rendangs — especially the Rendang Rembau — though time-consuming to prepare, are unsurpassed in taste and flavour.

A pleasant 32 kilometre drive from Seremban will take you into the heart of Port Dickson, a cosy, spruce and orderly seaside resort with friendly people and little traffic. Its tranquillity is frequently invaded by weekend visitors who descend on the town in search of brief respite from the urban life of nearby Kuala Lumpur and surrounding cities. As if not to disappoint holiday-makers, Port Dickson has, besides the serenity and solitude of golden beaches, lots more attractions, food being no exception. As in most seaside resorts throughout Malaysia, seafood is readily available in the clusters of foodstalls and the handful of restaurants in and around town. They are hardly cheap but the quality of freshness is wonderful. For noodle lovers, Port Dickson boasts several specialties like Lor Mee, Sang Meen and Fried Mee Sua — all delectable delights to savour.

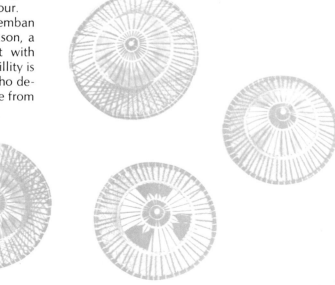

Opposite: Udang Goreng Cili Padi

Ikan Sembilang Masak Lemak Cili Padi

Preparation: 10 minutes   Cooking: 15 minutes

**450 g (1 lb) catfish, cut into
    5 cm (2 in) thick slices**
1 teaspoon salt

Ground Ingredients
20 bird chillies
2½ cm (1 in) ginger
2½ cm (1 in) turmeric root
7 shallots
2 cloves garlic

**1 turmeric leaf, torn through lengthwise
    to get full fragrance**
2 pieces dried tamarind skin
**1 coconut, grated (for 1 cup thick
    coconut milk and 2 cups thin
    coconut milk)**
½ teaspoon salt

Rub fish with salt and leave for 15 minutes.

Put ground ingredients, turmeric leaf, dried tamarind skin and thin coconut milk in a pot and bring to a slow boil, stirring frequently. Put in fish and simmer for 12 minutes until gravy is thick. Add thick coconut milk and salt to taste. Serve with boiled white rice.

Udang Goreng Cili Padi

(photograph on page 44)

Preparation: 10 minutes   Cooking: 8 minutes

**12 medium-large prawns, feelers
    and legs trimmed**
1 teaspoon salt
½ teaspoon sugar
4 tablespoons oil
30 bird chillies
2½ cm (1 in) turmeric root   } *ground*
3 cloves garlic
½ teaspoon turmeric powder
3 onions, sliced
2 heaped teaspoons tamarind paste   } *mixed and*
¼ cup water   *strained*
½ teaspoon salt
½ teaspoon monosodium glutamate
1 red chilli, seeded and sliced

Season prawns with salt and sugar and leave for 15 minutes.

Heat oil in a *kuali* and fry ground ingredients and turmeric powder for a minute, then add onions and fry until transparent and fragrant.

Add tamarind juice and bring to a boil. Put in prawns and stir-fry for 2 minutes. Cover *kuali* for 3 minutes. Uncover, add salt and monosodium glutamate and lastly sliced chilli.

Serve hot with rice.

Daging Masak Cili Padi

Preparation: 15 minutes   Cooking: 40 minutes

600 g (1 ⅓ lb) beef, cut into thin 4 cm
  (1 ½ in) slices

Ground Ingredients
30 bird chillies
2½ cm (1 in) turmeric root
2½ cm (1 in) ginger
1¼ cm (½ in) galingale
12 shallots
6 cloves garlic
2 stalks lemon grass, sliced

1½ coconuts, grated (for 5 cups
  coconut milk)
2 heaped tablespoons white grated coconut
  for 'kerisik'
1½ teaspoons salt

Score meat before cutting into slices.

Put meat, ground ingredients and coconut milk into a pot and bring to a boil. Simmer gently for 30 minutes until meat is tender. Put in *kerisik* and salt to taste and simmer for a further 5-10 minutes until gravy is thick.

Rendang Minangkabau

(photograph on page 51)

Preparation: 20 minutes   Cooking: 1½ hours

1 kg (2⅕ lb) beef, cut into 6 mm
  (¼ in) thick slices

Ground Ingredients
25 dried chillies, soaked
10 bird chillies
2½ cm (1 in) galingale
2½ cm (1 in) ginger
2½ cm (1 in) turmeric root
2 stalks lemon grass
15 shallots
10 cloves garlic

2 white coconuts, grated (4 tablespoons
  reserved for 'kerisik', 6 cups coconut
  milk from the rest)
2 stalks lemon grass, crushed lightly
1 piece dried tamarind skin
2 teaspoons salt
3 tablespoons oil
8 shallots ⎤
          ⎬ *sliced*
4 cloves garlic ⎦

Marinate beef with ground ingredients in a pot and leave for 15 minutes.

Pour in coconut milk and bring to a slow boil. Add the crushed lemon grass and dried tamarind skin and simmer over low heat, stirring frequently until gravy is quite thick.

Add *kerisik* and continue simmering, stirring all the time until meat is tender and gravy thick. Stir in salt to taste. In a separate saucepan, heat 3 tablespoons oil and brown shallots and garlic and add to Rendang.

Rendang Rembau

(photograph on page 51)

Preparation: 30 minutes   Cooking: 2 hours

1 kg (2¹/₅ lb) beef, cut into 5 cm
   (2 in) slices

Ground Ingredients
1 cup coriander, roasted
1 tablespoon black
   peppercorns, toasted   } *ground coarsely*
30 dried chillies, soaked
2½ cm (1 in) turmeric root
2½ cm (1 in) ginger   } *ground finely*
3 slices galingale

3 stalks lemon grass, crushed
12 shallots, sliced
5 cloves garlic, sliced
1 cup white grated coconut for 'kerisik',
   ground coarsely
3 cups water
1½ coconuts, grated (for 3 cups
   coconut milk)
2 teaspoons salt
3 tablespoons oil

Season beef with ground ingredients for 15 minutes. Put seasoned beef, crushed lemon grass, shallots, garlic, *kerisik* and water in a *kuali*. Bring to a boil, then lower heat and cook for 40 minutes, stirring occasionally.

At the end of that time, add coconut milk, return to a boil and simmer over low heat for 40 minutes, stirring all the time to ensure mixture does not stick to pan. When almost dry and meat appears oily, lower heat further. Add salt and lastly oil and continue stirring for approximately 20-25 minutes until beef is dark brown and truly dry.

Note: Coriander seeds and black peppercorns can either be placed in a moderate oven for 20-25 minutes, stirring occasionally for even toasting, or pan-fried over medium heat for over 5 minutes until fragrant. Please do not forget to wash coriander seeds in lots of water before toasting. You'll be amazed to find the great amount of grit settling at the bottom of the container.

To save time, coriander seeds, black peppercorns and kerisik can be milled dry.

Rendang Rembau is dry and looks dark brown. It tastes deliciously different and almost crisp out of the pan. It can be stored for a couple of weeks.

Sambal Tempoyak

Preparation: 10 minutes   Cooking: 15 minutes

4 tablespoons fermented durian
1 coconut, grated (for 'pati santan')
30 g (1 oz) dried anchovies,
   heads and entrails removed
30 bird chillies
2½ cm (1 in) turmeric root   } *ground together*
5 stalks lemon grass, ground separately
salt to taste

Mix all ingredients except ground lemon grass and salt in a pot and bring to a slow boil.

Add ground lemon grass and salt to taste and simmer gently for 10 minutes or until thick.

Serve with boiled white rice.

Rendang Ayam Negri Sembilan

Preparation: 20 minutes   Cooking: 45 minutes

1½ kg (3⅓ lb) chicken
1 teaspoon salt
12 shallots, sliced
6 cloves garlic, sliced

Ground Ingredients
20 dried chillies, soaked
20 bird chillies
2½ cm (1 in) ginger
2½ cm (1 in) galingale

2 stalks lemon grass, crushed lightly
1½ coconuts, grated (for 4 cups thick
   coconut milk)
2 turmeric leaves
4 tablespoons white grated coconut
   for 'kerisik'
1½ teaspoons salt

Marinate chicken with salt, sliced shallots and garlic, ground ingredients and lightly crushed lemon grass for 30 minutes.

Put marinated meat together with coconut milk in a pot and bring to a slow boil. Put in turmeric leaves and simmer gently, stirring constantly until gravy is thick. Stir in *kerisik* and salt to taste and simmer until chicken is tender and very little gravy remains.

Sambal Tempoyak Petai

Preparation: 35 minutes   Cooking: 15 minutes

2 tablespoons oil
45 g (1½ oz) dried **anchovies,**
   heads and entrails removed
1 coconut, grated (for 2¼ cups
   coconut milk)
2 onions, sliced

Ground Ingredients
20 red chillies
20 bird chillies
2 stalks lemon grass, sliced
2½ cm (1 in) turmeric root

3 tablespoons fermented durian
4 turmeric leaves   ⎤
10 tender tapioca leaves   ⎬ sliced
10 young pumpkin leaves   ⎦ finely
6-8 pods 'petai'
½ teaspoon salt or to taste

Heat oil in a cooking pot and lightly brown anchovies. Pour in coconut milk and add onions, ground ingredients and fermented durian. Bring to a slow boil, stirring at the same time. Add finely sliced leaves and simmer over low heat for 10 minutes. Extract *petai* seeds from pods and peel off hard skin. Add *petai* and salt and simmer for another 5 minutes until gravy thickens.

Note: Tempoyak goes very well with rice. For those not too familiar with the dish, it may taste unusual, but it is not difficult to acquire a liking for it.

Lemang (Bamboo Glutinous Rice Rolls)

(photograph opposite)

Preparation: 1 hour   Cooking: 4 hours

4 kg (9 lb) glutinous rice
4 tablespoons coarse salt
5 coconuts, grated (for sufficient
   coconut milk to cover rice)
24-26 green bamboos
   (see diagrams)
24-26 young banana leaves, long
   edges trimmed, cut into pieces 5 cm
   (2 in) longer than bamboos
firewood

Note: Lemang is a firm Hari Raya favourite and it is usually prepared by the elders in the kampung *where bamboo and firewood are readily available. It is so important with most* kampung *folk that wives would quarrel bitterly with their husbands if glutinous rice is not purchased for this speciality to celebrate Hari Raya.*

Lemang will keep well for 3-4 days without refrigeration if the glutinous rice is thoroughly washed until the water is clear.

Wash glutinous rice thoroughly and leave to soak for 1 hour. Drain and put rice in a large container. Add salt and enough coconut milk to cover rice completely. Mix well to dissolve salt.

Line each stick of bamboo with banana leaf (underside rolled in). This can be done easily with a banana leaf stem split through three-quarters down. Clip the long edge of the leaf in between the split banana stem, then roll up tightly (see diagrams). Thread into hollow bamboo. Carefully remove the banana stem, then stamp the bamboo on the ground to ensure that the banana leaf goes right down to the bottom.

Using a dessertspoon, fill four-fifths of the lined bamboo with rice and just enough coconut milk to cover rice. Stamp the filled bamboo a couple of times on the ground to firmly pack the rice. Fold and tuck in the top end of banana leaf to seal rice. Start a fire. Place bamboos in a neat row against a steel pole two-thirds of a metre (2 feet) away from the fire and cook for 3½-4 hours, turning bamboos frequently to prevent burning. While turning the bamboos, stamp again a couple of times to pack rice firmly.

When rice is cooked, split the bamboos with a sharp knife. Cut glutinous rice rolls into 2½ cm (1 in) thick pieces. Serve with your favourite Rendangs.

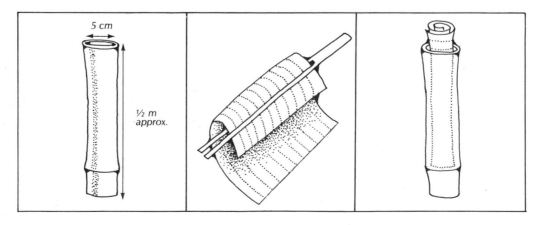

5 cm

½ m
approx.

Opposite: Lemang with Rendang Minangkabau (right) and Rendang Rembau (left)

Sang Meen

Preparation: 20 minutes   Cooking: 15 minutes   Serves: 3

300 g (10 oz) fresh egg noodles
   ('wan tan meen')
1 tablespoon oil
1 teaspoon sesame oil

Sauce Ingredients

150 g (5 oz) chicken or pork, cut into strips
240 g (8 oz) small prawns, shelled
120 g (4 oz) small-medium cuttlefish,
   cut into 1¼ cm (½ in) pieces
1½ teaspoons salt
1½ teaspoons sesame oil
pepper
3 tablespoons oil
3 cloves garlic, minced
2 cups anchovy or fresh chicken stock
½ tablespoon light soy sauce ⎫
½ teaspoon salt   ⎬ combined
½ teaspoon monosodium   ⎭
   glutamate
1 leaf long Chinese cabbage,
   cut into 6 mm (¼ in) strips
2-3 stalks mustard green, cut into
   5 cm (2 in) lengths
¼ cup water or stock   ⎫ combined
1½ tablespoons cornflour   ⎭

3-4 red chillies, sliced   ⎫ combined
2 tablespoons light soy sauce ⎭

Bring half a saucepan of water to a rapid boil. Scald noodles for under a minute. Drain with a large wiremesh noodle ladle and immediately dip into a basin of cool water for a few seconds. Re-scald noodles in boiling water again for a few seconds. Drain well and place in a deep dish. Mix in oil and sesame oil. Leave noodles aside to prepare sauce.

Season meat, prawns and cuttlefish separately with ½ teaspoon salt, ½ teaspoon sesame oil and a dash of pepper. Leave preferably for 15 minutes.

Heat 3 tablespoons oil in a *kuali* and brown garlic. Put in meat and stir-fry over high heat for 1 minute. Add prawns then cuttlefish. Stir-fry until cooked. Dish out and leave aside.

Pour stock into *kuali*, add combined seasoning ingredients and bring to a rapid boil. Add Chinese cabbage and mustard greens—stems first. When just cooked, put in fried meat, prawns and cuttlefish. Allow to boil again then stir in cornflour thickening.

Pour boiling hot sauce over noodles and serve immediately with combined chillies and light soy sauce.

Fried Mee Sua

Preparation: 30 minutes   Cooking: 15 minutes   Serves: 5

oil for deep-frying
300 g (10 oz) fine rice vermicelli
  ('mee sua'), left unwashed
450 g (1 lb) beansprouts, tailed
6 cups water
3 tablespoons oil
5 shallots, sliced
4 cloves garlic, minced
150 g (5 oz) chicken or pork,
  cut into strips
300 g (10 oz) small prawns, shelled
1 teaspoon salt
1 teaspoon pepper
3 cups anchovy or chicken stock
4 stalks mustard green, cut into
  5 cm (2 in) lengths
2 tablespoons light soy sauce
½ teaspoon monosodium glutamate
2 stalks spring onion   *cut into 2½ cm*
1 sprig coriander leaves   *(1 in) lengths*
3-4 red chillies, sliced
2 tablespoons light soy sauce   *combined*

Heat oil for deep-frying (approximately 3 cups) in a *kuali* until hot. Put in vermicelli, a bundle at a time, and fry, turning over very quickly with chopsticks until light golden. Vermicelli will sizzle in hot oil—remove as soon as it stops sizzling. This takes only 15 seconds. Drain in a colander.

Remove oil, leaving 3 tablespoonfuls in the *kuali*. Put in beansprouts and fry for 1 minute. Dish out and leave aside.

Pour 6 cups water into the *kuali* and bring to a boil. Put in the fried vermicelli and cook for 1-2 minutes until soft. Immediately pour vermicelli into a colander and drain well.

Heat 3 tablespoons oil in a *kuali* and brown shallots and garlic. Put in chicken and stir-fry for 2 minutes, then add prawns, salt and pepper. When cooked, dish out and leave aside.

Pour anchovy or chicken stock into the *kuali* and bring to a boil. Throw in mustard greens, stems first, then add light soy sauce and monosodium glutamate and cook for 1 minute. Add vermicelli, beansprouts, fried meat and prawns, and mix well.

Throw in spring onions and coriander leaves and serve hot with sliced red chillies and light soy sauce.

Lor Mee

Preparation: 30 minutes   Cooking: 15 minutes   Serves: 6

300 g (10 oz) chicken or pork,
  cut into strips
450 g (1 lb) small prawns, shelled
300 g (10 oz) small-medium cuttlefish,
  cleaned
1½ teaspoons salt
1½ teaspoons pepper
3 teaspoons light soy sauce
4 tablespoons oil
5 shallots, sliced
5 cloves garlic, minced
7 cups anchovy or fresh
  chicken stock
1 carrot, cut into 5 cm
  (2 in) strips
4 leaves long Chinese cabbage, cut into
  1¼ cm (½ in) strips
2 dessertspoons light soy sauce
½ teaspoon dark soy sauce
12 fishballs
1 kg (2¹/₅ lb) fresh yellow
  noodles
4 tablespoons black vinegar
1 teaspoon salt
½ teaspoon monosodium glutamate
3 tablespoons cornflour ⎫ combined
½ cup water ⎭
2 eggs, beaten lightly
2 stalks spring onion, chopped
2 sprigs coriander leaves, chopped
3-4 red chillies, sliced ⎫ combined
2 tablespoons light soy sauce ⎭

Marinate chicken, prawns and cuttlefish separately with ½ teaspoon salt, ½ teaspoon pepper and 1 teaspoon light soy sauce.

Heat oil in a *kuali* and brown shallots and garlic. Add chicken and stir-fry for 2 minutes, then put in prawns and cuttlefish. Stir-fry until just cooked. Dish out and keep aside.

Pour anchovy or chicken stock into *kuali* and bring to a boil. Put in carrot and cabbage leaves, light and dark soy sauces, and fishballs. Simmer for 5 minutes. Add noodles and bring to a slow boil over moderate heat. Stir in black vinegar, salt, monosodium glutamate and thickening. Drizzle in beaten eggs over boiling gravy, stir gently and lastly add spring onions and coriander leaves.

Serve hot with sliced chillies and light soy sauce or Sambal Belacan (page 82).

Dodol

Preparation: 15 minutes   Cooking: 2½ hours

1 kg (2¹/₅ lb) glutinous rice
    flour
4 coconuts, grated (for 7 cups
    coconut milk)
700 g (1½ lb) palm sugar,
    chopped
240 g (8 oz) sugar   *boiled to*
1 cup water   *dissolve sugar*
3 screwpine leaves, knotted

Put glutinous rice flour into a bowl and blend with coconut milk until smooth. Strain mixture into a large non-stick pan and cook over low heat, stirring all the time with a wooden spoon until mixture starts to thicken.

Strain palm sugar syrup into flour mixture and continue stirring for 2 hours until mixture turns into an oily lump of dark brown dough.

Put dodol into a *mengkuang* (screwpine mat) basket. If this is not available put into two 15 x 25 cm (6 x 10 in) ungreased pyrex dishes. Smooth surface with a plastic spatula and cool completely, preferably overnight, before cutting.

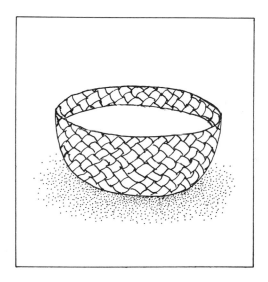

SELANGOR.

When one talks of Selangor, invariably the discussion drifts to Kuala Lumpur, formerly the state capital of Selangor. (The new state capital is Shah Alam.)

Kuala Lumpur the capital city throbs with vitality, and although more than a hundred years old, it is a melting pot of inhabitants from other States and towns in Malaysia. Which is probably why it is a veritable gourmet's paradise with some of the best cosmopolitan cuisines in the nation. The cluster of international hotels in the 'Golden Triangle' cater authentic Malay, Chinese and Indian as well as international cuisines.

Malay food is a rich mixture of the curries and hot sambals from north to south Peninsular Malaysia. Even the most discerning of gourmets will find the range wide and enticing, some still waiting to be discovered.

The variety of Chinese dishes to be encountered in Kuala Lumpur is amazing. Every provincial variety, cooked to perfection, is available here, be it Cantonese (Guangdong), Hokkien (Fujian), Hakka, Teochew (Chaozhou), Hainanese, Shanghainese, Peking (Beijing), Taiwanese or Szechuan (Sichuan).

First-class restaurants may be found throughout Kuala Lumpur and Selangor, but one should not ignore the food stalls that do a roaring trade catering to the local populace with favourites like Bak Kut Teh and the typically 'KL' Hokkien Mee.

Opposite: Fish Bladders Topped with Prawns and Fried Soybean Cake with Chilli

Fish Head Curry

Preparation: 15 minutes   Cooking: 25 minutes

1 fish head (approx. 1 kg/2¹/₅ lb)
1 teaspoon salt
8 tablespoons oil

Ground Ingredients
25 dried chillies
12 shallots
2 cloves garlic
3 stalks lemon grass, sliced
2½ cm (1 in) galingale
2½ cm (1 in) square dried shrimp
   paste

30 g (1 oz) fish curry powder | *mixed to*
3 tablespoons water | *a paste*
90 g (3 oz) tamarind paste | *mixed and*
1 cup water | *strained*
1 coconut, grated (for 3 cups
   coconut milk)
10 lady's fingers
3 tomatoes, halved
5 red chillies
5 green chillies
1 teaspoon sugar
1½ teaspoons salt

Clean fish head thoroughly and rub with salt.

Heat oil in a *kuali* and fry ground ingredients for 3 minutes, then add curry powder paste and fry until fragrant and oil separates.

Add strained tamarind juice and coconut milk and bring to a boil. Lower heat and simmer for 5 minutes. Put in lady's fingers, then tomatoes, red and green chillies and simmer for 5 minutes. Add sugar and salt and lastly fish head. Cook for 10 minutes until fish is done.

Serve hot with boiled white rice.

Stuffed Horse Mackerel

Preparation: 10 minutes   Cooking: 8 minutes

3 large horse mackerels
1½ teaspoons salt

Ground Ingredients
90 g (3 oz) dried prawns, washed
   and drained dry
6 red chillies
2½ cm (1 in) square dried shrimp
   paste
1 stalk lemon grass
8 shallots
2 cloves garlic

4-5 tablespoons oil
1 small head lettuce

Clean and remove the hard outer skin from fish. Make deep slits on both sides of the fish parallel to the backbone, taking care not to cut right through. Rub fish with salt and put ground ingredients into the slits and cavities of fish.

Heat oil in a *kuali* until hot. Cook for 3-4 minutes on one side, then turn fish and fry for another 3-4 minutes until well browned. Remove and drain well. Serve hot on a bed of lettuce.

Fish Bladders Topped with Prawns

(photograph on page 56)

Preparation: 25 minutes   Steaming: 12 minutes   Cooking: 5 minutes

75 g (2½ oz) dried fish bladders
oil for deep-frying
1 teaspoon alkaline water
1 kg (2¹⁄₅ lb) prawns, shelled
   and minced
1 egg white
½ teaspoon salt
¼ teaspoon pepper
crab roe
1 tablespoon oil
1 dessertspoon rice wine
240 g (8 oz) crabmeat
8-10 button mushrooms, sliced
10 snow peas or 90 g (3 oz) peas

Sauce
1 cup fresh chicken stock
½ teaspoon salt
¼ teaspoon pepper
pinch of monosodium glutamate
1 teaspoon cornflour
1 egg white, beaten lightly

coriander leaves

Dry fish bladders in the sun for 1 hour and deep-fry until puffy. Soak in a basin of water until soft. (As fish bladders are light, it is necessary to weight them down.) Cut into matchbox-size pieces. There should be approximately 24 pieces. Drain, add alkaline water and mix well, then wash thoroughly with water. Squeeze dry and leave aside. Hard pieces, if any, should be discarded.

Season prawns with egg white, salt and pepper and beat with a spoon until mixture is sticky.

Spread a spoonful of minced prawns over surface of each fish bladder. Top with a little crab roe. If this is not available, substitute with a little minced carrot.

Steam fish bladders in a steamer for 12 minutes.

Heat 1 tablespoon oil in a *kuali*, add rice wine, then put in crabmeat, mushrooms, snow peas or peas and stir-fry for 1-2 minutes. Add sauce ingredients and bring to a boil. As soon as it thickens, spoon half of the sauce over fish bladders.

Stir beaten egg white into remaining gravy and when it boils again, pour over fish bladders. Serve hot, garnished with coriander leaves.

Fish Slices with Cauliflower

Preparation: 20 minutes   Cooking: 15 minutes

600 g (1⅓ lb) threadfin,
    central portion
1 egg, beaten lightly
1 teaspoon cornflour
1 teaspoon salt
oil for deep-frying
240 g (8 oz) cauliflower, cut into
    pieces
6 cloves garlic, minced
10 slices carrot, parboiled
1 stalk leek, green portion discarded,
    cut into 5 cm (2 in) lengths
½ can (365 g/12 oz) button mushrooms,
    halved
1 teaspoon rice wine
1 tablespoon light soy sauce
½ tablespoon oyster sauce
1 teaspoon dark soy sauce } *combined*
½ teaspoon monosodium
    glutamate
¼ teaspoon pepper
¾ cup fresh chicken stock
¼ teaspoon sesame oil
½ teaspoon salt
1 tablespoon peas
1 heaped teaspoon cornflour
1 tablespoon water } *combined*
1 stalk spring onion, chopped

Cut fish into 1¼ x 2½ x 4 cm (½ x 1 x 1½ in) pieces. Marinate with egg, cornflour and salt.

Heat oil for deep-frying in a *kuali*. Put in cauliflower and stir-fry for 10 seconds. Remove and leave aside.

Put in fish slices and fry for 1 minute. Remove and keep aside.

Leave 1 tablespoon oil in the *kuali* and lightly brown garlic. Put in fried cauliflower, carrot, leek and mushrooms and fry for 2 minutes. Add combined sauces then fish. Pour in stock and bring to a quick boil. Add sesame oil, salt to taste, and lastly peas. Thicken with cornflour mixture and serve hot sprinkled with spring onion.

Sweet and Sour Fish

Preparation: 10 minutes Cooking: 20 minutes

600 g (1 ⅓ lb) grouper, two slits made
   across fish on each side
1 ½ teaspoons salt
1 ½ tablespoons cornflour
oil for deep-frying

Sauce Ingredients
1 ½ tablespoons oil
4 cloves garlic, minced
2 onions, cut into wedges
2 red chillies, cut into strips
2 slices ginger, cut into strips
2 cups water ⎫
3 tablespoons tomato sauce ⎪
2 tablespoons chilli sauce ⎬ *combined*
1 tablespoon sugar ⎪
½ teaspoon salt ⎭
1 cucumber, soft portion removed,
   cut into wedges
2 tomatoes, cut into wedges
1 ½ tablespoons cornflour ⎫ *combined*
2 tablespoons water ⎭
½ tablespoon plum sauce

coriander leaves
spring onion leaves

Rub fish with salt and cornflour.

Heat oil in a *kuali* until hot. Put in fish and deep-fry for 15 minutes until fish is cooked and golden. Drain and place on an oval dish.

Sauce
Heat oil in a *kuali* and put in garlic, onions, chillies and ginger. Fry for a minute then add combined sauces. When it comes to a boil, put in cucumber, tomatoes and cornflour thickening. Lastly stir in plum sauce.

To Serve
Pour sauce over fish. Serve hot garnished with coriander leaves and spring onions.

Sharksfin Soup

Preparation: 20 minutes Cooking: 6 minutes

600 g (1 ⅓ lb) crabs, preferably with roe,
   steamed, meat and roe separated
2 eggs ⎫ *beaten*
2 tablespoons water ⎭ *lightly*
2 tablespoons corn oil
1 tablespoon rice wine
2 cups fresh chicken stock
180 g (6 oz) pre-prepared sharksfin,
   washed and drained
1 teaspoon salt
1 dessertspoon light soy sauce
½ teaspoon pepper
½ teaspoon monosodium glutamate
2 tablespoons cornflour ⎫ *combined*
2 tablespoons water ⎭
1 tablespoon corn oil

Mince crab roe and stir into beaten egg mixture. Leave aside.

Heat corn oil in a *kuali* until hot. Add rice wine, then chicken stock and bring to a boil. Put in sharksfin, stir well, then add salt, light soy sauce, pepper, monosodium glutamate and crabmeat.

When it comes to a boil again, thicken with cornflour mixture and let it simmer over low heat. Gradually, stir in beaten egg mixture and lastly add 1 tablespoon corn oil. Serve immediately.

Scrambled Eggs Sharksfin

Preparation: 15 minutes   Cooking: 6 minutes

180 g (6 oz) pre-prepared sharksfin
180 g (6 oz) cooked crabmeat
**60 g (2 oz) steamed or boiled chicken
     meat, cut into strips**
6 eggs
1 tablespoon corn oil
1 teaspoon pepper
1 teaspoon salt
1 dessertspoon light soy sauce
1 dessertspoon rice wine
½ teaspoon monosodium glutamate
6 tablespoons oil
**60 g (2 oz) beansprouts, heads and tails
     pinched off**
**1 stalk spring onion, cut into 2½ cm
     (1 in) lengths**
2 sprigs coriander leaves
1-2 heads lettuce

Wash sharksfin and drain well.

Put sharksfin, crabmeat, chicken, eggs, corn oil, pepper, salt, light soy sauce, rice wine and monosodium glutamate in a mixing bowl and mix well.

Heat 1 tablespoon of the oil in a *kuali* until very hot and fry beansprouts for a minute. Remove and leave aside.

Heat another tablespoon of the oil in the *kuali* and pour in egg mixture. Scramble gently and at the same time add remaining oil, a tablespoon at a time. When egg mixture is almost cooked, put in beansprouts and spring onion. Stir-fry to mix well.

Garnish with coriander leaves. Serve hot with lettuce.

Chilli Oyster Crabs

(photograph opposite)

Preparation: 15 minutes   Cooking: 20 minutes

3 kg (6²/₃ lb) crabs
1 cup oil
**60 g (2 oz) ginger, cut into
     strips**
7 cloves garlic, sliced
7 shallots, sliced
10 red chillies, seeded ⎫ *machine-*
½ cup water ⎭ *blended*

Sauce Ingredients
3 tablespoons rice wine
3 tablespoons chilli sauce
4 tablespoons oyster sauce
4 dessertspoons sugar
1 teaspoon light soy sauce
1 teaspoon sesame oil
½ teaspoon monosodium glutamate
¼ teaspoon pepper

5 eggs, beaten lightly
6 stalks spring onion ⎫ *cut into 5 cm*
2 sprigs coriander leaves ⎭ *(2 in) lengths*

Clean crabs and remove and crack pincers with a pestle. Trim legs and cut each crab into four pieces.

Heat oil in a large *kuali* and stir-fry ginger, garlic and shallots until fragrant. Put in ground chillies and fry for 2 minutes.

Put in crabs and stir briskly. Cover *kuali* for approximately 4-5 minutes. Uncover and stir briskly once again, then add sauce ingredients. When crabs are bright red and nearly cooked, pour in beaten eggs. Add spring onions, stirring to mix with sauce.

Dish out and serve hot, garnished with coriander leaves.

Opposite: Chilli Oyster Crabs

Prawn and Pineapple Curry

Preparation: 15 minutes Cooking: 15 minutes

12 large prawns
5 tablespoons oil
2 stalks lemon grass, crushed lightly

Ground Ingredients
8 red chillies
15 shallots
5 cm (2 in) galingale
2½ cm (1 in) turmeric root
2½ cm (1 in) square dried
   shrimp paste
3 candlenuts

½ small ripe pineapple, sliced
1 coconut, grated (for 1 cup thick
   coconut milk and 2 cups thin
   coconut milk)
1½ teaspoons salt

Wash and trim off feelers and legs of prawns. Leave shells intact.

Heat oil in a *kuali* and fry crushed lemon grass and ground ingredients until fragrant and oil separates.

Add pineapple then thin coconut milk. Bring to a slow boil then simmer gently for 5 minutes. Put in prawns and simmer until almost cooked then add thick coconut milk and salt and simmer until prawns are thoroughly cooked.

Prawn Sambal

Preparation: 20 minutes Cooking: 20 minutes

600 g (1⅓ lb) prawns, shelled
   and deveined
1 teaspoon salt
5 tablespoons oil
2 onions, sliced
4 cloves garlic, sliced

Ground Ingredients
10 dried chillies, soaked or
   2 teaspoons chilli powder
6 red chillies
2½ cm (1 in) turmeric root
2 teaspoons coriander
1 teaspoon cummin
6 black peppercorns
½ teaspoon fenugreek

1 heaped teaspoon tamarind paste | *mixed and*
4 tablespoons water | *strained*
2 tomatoes, cut into wedges
1 coconut, grated (for 1 cup 'pati
   santan')
1½ teaspoons salt

Rub prawns with salt, then wash and drain in a colander.

Heat oil in a *kuali* and lightly brown onions and garlic for 2-3 minutes. Add ground ingredients and fry until fragrant and oil separates.

Put in tamarind juice and tomatoes and simmer gently for 10 minutes. Add the prawns, then *pati santan* and salt to taste. Bring to a boil over low heat, stirring constantly until prawns are cooked. Serve with boiled white rice.

Plum Sauce Prawns

Preparation: 10 minutes   Cooking: 8 minutes

5 tablespoons oil
600 g (1⅓ lb) large prawns,
     feelers trimmed
5 cm (2 in) ginger, chopped
4 cloves garlic, minced
1 dessertspoon dark soy sauce ⎫
1 dessertspoon light soy sauce ⎬ combined
1 dessertspoon sugar   ⎪
1 teaspoon salt   ⎭
1 tablespoon plum sauce
2 sprigs coriander leaves ⎫ chopped
2 stalks spring onion   ⎭

Heat oil in a *kuali* until hot. Put in prawns and fry for 2 minutes until they turn red. Remove and drain.

Scoop out oil, leaving 2 tablespoonfuls in *kuali*. Brown ginger and garlic, then put in prawns. Stir-fry and add combined seasoning. Stir-fry quickly till prawns are cooked, then add plum sauce and lastly coriander leaves and spring onions.

Dish out and serve hot.

Crispy Prawn Fritters

Preparation: 15 minutes Cooking: 15 minutes

600 g (1⅓ lb) large prawns

Seasoning Ingredients
½ teaspoon bicarbonate of soda
½ teaspoon salt
1 teaspoon sugar
1 teaspoon monosodium glutamate
½ egg white
1 tablespoon cornflour
1 dessertspoon oil

Batter Ingredients
120 g (4 oz) self-raising flour
240 g (8 oz) rice flour
1½ teaspoons baking powder
½ teaspoon sugar
½ teaspoon salt
½ teaspoon monosodium glutamate
1½ cups water
½ teaspoon tabasco sauce

oil for deep-frying

Sweet Sour Chilli Sauce
4 tablespoons chilli sauce   ⎫
1 tablespoon tomato sauce   ⎪
juice of 5 small limes   ⎪
2 tablespoons plum sauce   ⎬ combined
2 tablespoons sugar   ⎪
1 dessertspoon A1 sauce   ⎪
¼ teaspoon salt   ⎪
1 clove garlic, ground   ⎭

Shell prawns, leaving tails behind. Devein and dry with a piece of cloth. Mix well with bicarbonate of soda, salt, sugar and monosodium glutamate, then add egg white, cornflour and cooking oil. Season for at least half an hour.

To make batter, sift both kinds of flour and baking powder into a mixing bowl, add sugar, salt and monosodium glutamate. Make a well in the centre and gradually blend in water until batter is of a smooth consistency. It should be slightly thick and not too runny. Stir in tabasco sauce.

Heat oil for deep-frying in a *kuali*. Dip seasoned prawns in thick batter and fry till golden brown. Drain on absorbent paper. Put prawns on a serving plate garnished with cucumber and tomato slices. Serve hot with Sweet Sour Chilli Sauce.

Prawn Curry

Preparation: 10 minutes Cooking: 12-15 minutes

12 large prawns, shells left intact,
  feelers and legs trimmed

Ground Ingredients
10 red chillies
12 shallots
4 cloves garlic
2 stalks lemon grass, sliced
2½ cm (1 in) turmeric root
1¼ cm (½ in) galingale
4 candlenuts

5 tablespoons oil
1½ teaspoons salt
1 coconut, grated (for 1 cup thick
  coconut milk and 2 cups thin
  coconut milk)

Season prawns with ground ingredients and leave for 30 minutes.

Heat oil in a *kuali*, add prawns and fry for 3-4 minutes. Put in salt and thin coconut milk and bring to a boil. Lower heat and add thick coconut milk. Simmer, stirring frequently, until prawns are cooked.

Yim Kok Har (Fried Salted Prawns)

Preparation: 10 minutes   Cooking: 5 minutes

600 g (1⅓ lb) large prawns
3 cups water
3 teaspoons salt
1 heaped teaspoon five-spice powder
1 egg white, beaten lightly
½ teaspoon salt
¼ teaspoon pepper
½ teaspoon monosodium glutamate
2 tablespoons cornflour ⎫
1 tablespoon rice flour ⎪
1 tablespoon flour   ⎬ *sifted together*
¼ teaspoon five-spice   ⎪
  powder   ⎪
pinch of pepper   ⎭
oil for deep-frying
½ cucumber ⎫ *sliced*
1 tomato   ⎭
coriander leaves

Wash prawns, leave shells on and trim feelers and legs. Put prawns in a bowl with 3 cups water or just enough to cover prawns. Stir in salt and five-spice powder and keep refrigerated for 2 hours.

Drain and dry prawns with a tea towel. Mix in beaten egg white, salt, pepper and monosodium glutamate.

Place sifted flour ingredients and seasoning in a bowl. Dip prawns in this to coat thoroughly with flour mixture.

Heat oil for deep-frying in a *kuali* and fry prawns till golden brown in colour. Serve garnished with cucumber and tomato slices and coriander leaves.

> *Note: Instead of dipping prawns in flour mixture, prawns can be placed on a flat tray, then combined flour mixture sifted carefully over prawns. Turn the prawns over and sift more flour mixture to coat prawns completely.*

Chinese Beef Steak

Preparation: 10 minutes   Cooking: 15 minutes

700 g (1½ lb) fillet steak

Seasoning Ingredients
2 teaspoons light soy sauce
1 teaspoon bicarbonate of soda
½ teaspoon salt
1 teaspoon monosodium glutamate
1 dessertspoon ginger juice
1 tablespoon sugar
1 tablespoon cornflour
1 egg, beaten lightly

5 tablespoons oil

Sauce
½ cup stock or water
2 tablespoons light soy sauce
½ tablespoon dark soy sauce
1 tablespoon oyster sauce
1 tablespoon sugar
½ teaspoon sesame oil
¼ teaspoon salt
¼ teaspoon pepper

1 dessertspoon cornflour ⎱ *combined*
2 tablespoons water ⎰
coriander leaves ⎱ *cut into 5 cm*
2 stalks spring onion ⎰ *(2 in) lengths*
1 red chilli, cut into strips

Cut fillet steak into 6 mm (¼ in) thick slices. Using the back of a cleaver, lightly score the meat to tenderize. Season beef with seasoning ingredients, adding the beaten egg last, and leave for 3 hours.

Heat oil in a *kuali* until hot. Fry beef until slightly brown on both sides. Remove and arrange on a dish.

Pour sauce ingredients into the *kuali* and bring to a boil. Thicken with cornflour mixture. Pour sauce over beef and serve hot, garnished with coriander leaves, spring onions and chilli strips.

Spicy Mutton Soup

Preparation: 10 minutes   Cooking: 2 hours

1 kg (2¹/₅ lb) mutton, fatty streaks
    removed, cut into 2½ cm (1 in) cubes
10 cups water
5 cm (2 in) stick cinnamon
8 cloves
2 whole star anise
1 teaspoon white peppercorns
½ teaspoon coriander
½ teaspoon fennel
½ teaspoon cummin
2 teaspoons salt
½ teaspoon monosodium glutamate
8 shallots ⎤ *sliced and*
3 cloves garlic ⎦ *fried crisp*
2 stalks spring onion, chopped

Put mutton and water in a pot and bring to a boil.

Lightly crush spices and tie up securely in a piece of white cloth.

Drop spice bag into boiling soup. Lower heat and simmer gently for 2 hours until meat is tender. Remove scum and add salt and monosodium glutamate.

Serve hot, garnished with shallot and garlic crisps and spring onions.

Pee Par Hup (Roasted Duck with Plum Sauce)   *(photograph opposite)*

Preparation: 5 minutes   Steaming: 1 hour   Cooking: 25 minutes

1 pre-roasted duck
oil for deep-frying
4 tablespoons oil

Sauce Ingredients
3 tablespoons tomato sauce
1 tablespoon chilli sauce
1 tablespoon plum sauce
2½ dessertspoons sugar
½ teaspoon salt
2 teaspoons sesame oil
3 dessertspoons A1 sauce
1½ dessertspoons Worcestershire sauce
5 tablespoons hot water
1 teaspoon cornflour

1 tablespoon roasted sesame seeds
coriander leaves

Put roasted duck in a steamer over rapidly boiling water and steam for 1 hour. If preferred, duck can be steamed the night before.

Cut across breast of duck lengthwise using a sharp cleaver.

Heat oil for deep-frying in a *kuali* until hot. Fry duck, turning over occasionally, for 15-20 minutes until skin is crisp and golden brown.

Cut duck into serving-size pieces and arrange neatly on a dish.

Heat 4 tablespoons oil in a *kuali* and add combined sauce ingredients. When sauce thickens, spoon over duck and sprinkle with roasted sesame seeds.

Serve hot, garnished with coriander leaves.

Opposite: Pee Par Hup

Crispy Skin Chicken

Preparation: 10 minutes   Cooking: 25 minutes

1½ kg (3⅓ lb) chicken
1 tablespoon salt
3 sticks cinnamon, each 7½ cm (3 in) long
juice of 10 small limes, strained
2 tablespoons malt ('mak gar tong')
1 teaspoon salt
oil for deep-frying
cucumber slices
tomato slices
prawn crackers

Clean chicken thoroughly and remove pancreas. Cut off feet. Break the thigh bone joints and carefully remove thigh bones from the inside with the help of a small knife. Leave drumstick bones intact.

Rub the inside of chicken with salt and place cinnamon sticks horizontally across in the stomach.

Making sure it is greaseless, bring half a *kuali* of water to boil. Tie neck of chicken firmly with a piece of strong string. Hold chicken just above rapidly boiling water and, using a ladle, scald chicken several times with boiling water. Throw water away and wash *kuali* thoroughly — there should be no grease. Bring another half *kuali* of water to a boil, add strained lime juice and stir in malt and salt until malt dissolves completely.

Dip and scald chicken in boiling malt water by turning chicken quickly in *kuali*. Remove chicken and hang in the sun to dry for 5 hours.

Heat oil for deep-frying in a *kuali* until hot and fry chicken for 15 minutes until golden brown. If chicken should brown too quickly, lower heat. Should air bubbles appear on chicken skin, prick with a skewer.

Cut chicken into serving size pieces and serve hot garnished with cucumber and tomato slices and top with prawn crackers.

Note: Pick a chicken with perfect skin, without a tear or slit, for this recipe.

Steamed Chicken Glutinous Rice

Preparation: 30 minutes Cooking: 15 minutes Steaming: 90 minutes

1½ kg (3⅓ lb) chicken

Seasoning Ingredients
4 tablespoons oyster sauce
2 teaspoons rice wine
1 teaspoon dark soy sauce
2 teaspoons light soy sauce
2 teaspoons ginger juice
1 teaspoon sesame oil
1 teaspoon sugar
½ teaspoon pepper
¼ teaspoon monosodium glutamate
1 heaped teaspoon cornflour

1 kg (2⅕ lb) glutinous rice
8 tablespoons oil
60 g (2 oz) dried Chinese mushrooms,
   soaked and cut into strips
8 shallots, sliced
2 teaspoons salt
1 teaspoon dark soy sauce
1 heaped teaspoon five-spice powder
4 cups water

Garnishing Ingredients
2 red chillies, seeded and sliced
2 stalks spring onion, chopped
4 sprigs coriander leaves, cut into
   2½ cm (1 in) lengths

Debone chicken and cut into 1¼ cm (½ in) thick slices. Season with seasoning ingredients for at least 1 hour.

Wash and drain glutinous rice and steam for 45 minutes.

Heat oil in a *kuali* and fry mushrooms for 1-2 minutes. Drain from oil and leave aside.

Lightly brown shallots and put in glutinous rice, salt, dark soy sauce and five-spice powder and fry for 1 minute. Add water, mix well and simmer gently, covered, for 5-10 minutes. Remove from heat.

Grease 12 medium rice bowls and put in some fried mushrooms and seasoned chicken at the bottom of each bowl. Fill with glutinous rice and press with the back of a spoon to fill three-quarters of rice bowl. Steam over rapidly boiling water for 45 minutes.

To serve, turn steamed glutinous rice onto a small dish. Garnish with chillies, spring onions and coriander leaves and serve hot with chilli sauce.

Chicken Rendang

Preparation: 15 minutes   Cooking: 40 minutes

1½ kg (3⅓ lb) chicken, cut into
   bite-size pieces
1 teaspoon salt
1 teaspoon black peppercorns, ground
½ cup oil

Ground Ingredients
15 dried chillies
150 g (5 oz) onions
150 g (5 oz) shallots
1 whole pod garlic
12 red chillies
4 cm (1½ in) turmeric root

3 stalks lemon grass, crushed lightly
1 coconut, grated (for 2 cups
   coconut milk)
1 teaspoon salt

Marinate chicken with salt and black pepper and leave for 30 minutes.

Heat oil in a *kuali* until hot and fry marinated chicken for 5 minutes until lightly browned.

Remove chicken with a perforated ladle, leaving oil in the *kuali*. Fry ground ingredients and lemon grass until fragrant and oil appears on the surface.

Lower heat, pour in coconut milk and bring to a slow boil. Add chicken and salt and simmer till chicken is tender and gravy thick.

Steamed Chicken Wings

Preparation: 10 minutes   Steaming: 12 minutes

6 pairs chicken wings, cut at the joints

Seasoning Ingredients
1 tablespoon light soy sauce
1 tablespoon oyster sauce
2 teaspoons cornflour
1 teaspoon sugar
1 teaspoon dark soy sauce
½ teaspoon salt
¼ teaspoon pepper
2½ cm (1 in) ginger, minced

1 tablespoon oil
2 dried Chinese mushrooms, soaked
   and sliced
2 red chillies, seeded and sliced
1 sprig coriander leaves ⎤ *chopped*
1 stalk spring onion ⎦

Wash and dry chicken wings thoroughly. Marinate with seasoning ingredients and 1 tablespoon oil and leave for 1 hour.

Place on a heatproof dish, sprinkle with sliced mushrooms and chillies and steam over rapidly boiling water for 12 minutes. Serve hot, sprinkled with chopped coriander leaves and spring onion.

Chicken and Assorted Mushrooms

Preparation: 15 minutes   Cooking: 10 minutes

½ **can (385 g/13 oz) button mushrooms, halved**
½ **can (425 g/15 oz) straw mushrooms, halved**
½ **can (425 g/15 oz) oyster or abalone mushrooms, halved**
7 dried Chinese mushrooms, halved
240 g (8 oz) chicken, cut into strips

Seasoning Ingredients
2 teaspoons light soy sauce
1 teaspoon salt
1 teaspoon sugar
¼ teaspoon pepper
¼ teaspoon monosodium glutamate
1 teaspoon sesame oil
2 teaspoons cornflour

5 tablespoons oil
3 cloves garlic, minced

Sauce
1 cup chicken stock
3 teaspoons oyster sauce
2 teaspoons light soy sauce
1 teaspoon sugar
½ teaspoon sesame oil
¼ teaspoon salt
¼ teaspoon pepper
¼ teaspoon monosodium glutamate
3 teaspoons cornflour

1 stalk spring onion
1 sprig coriander leaves } *chopped*
1 red chilli

Soak button mushrooms, straw mushrooms, oyster mushrooms and dried Chinese mushrooms separately in water for at least 15 minutes. Drain.

Season chicken with seasoning ingredients and leave aside.

Heat 1 tablespoon of the oil in a *kuali* until hot and stir-fry Chinese mushrooms until fragrant. Remove and leave aside.

Put 2 tablespoons oil in the *kuali,* lightly brown garlic, then add chicken and fry for 2 minutes. Remove and leave aside.

Heat remaining oil in the *kuali,* add button mushrooms, then straw and oyster mushrooms and stir-fry for 2 minutes. Add fried Chinese mushrooms and chicken and mix well.

Pour in prepared sauce and bring to a boil. When sauce thickens, add chopped spring onion, coriander leaves and chilli. Serve hot with rice.

Dry Chicken Curry

Preparation: 15 minutes   Cooking: 25 minutes

1 kg (2¹/₅ lb) chicken

Ground Ingredients
10 red chillies
10 dried chillies, soaked
15 shallots
8 cloves garlic
2½ cm (1 in) turmeric root

2 teaspoons salt
½ cup oil
1 coconut, grated (for 1 cup 'pati santan')
juice of 1 lemon or lime

Cut chicken into bite-size pieces and season with ground ingredients and salt. Leave aside for 3 hours.

Heat oil in a *kuali* and fry seasoned chicken until lightly browned. Add *pati santan* and simmer over low heat, stirring occasionally until chicken is tender and gravy dry. Just before dishing out, add lemon juice.

Paper-wrapped Chicken

Preparation: 10 minutes   Cooking: 15 minutes   Makes: 14 packages

1½ kg (3⅓ lb) chicken, cut into 14 large pieces

Seasoning Ingredients
2 sprigs coriander leaves ⎤
2 stalks spring onion ⎦ *chopped*
1 whole pod garlic, ground
juice from 5 cm (2 in) ginger
½ tablespoon rice wine
1 teaspoon five-spice powder
3 tablespoons oyster sauce
2 tablespoons light soy sauce
1 teaspoon sesame oil
1 teaspoon dark soy sauce
1 teaspoon salt
½ teaspoon sugar
½ teaspoon monosodium glutamate
½ teaspoon pepper
2 heaped tablespoons tapioca flour

greaseproof paper made into 10 x 15 cm (4 x 6 in) bags
1 tablespoon corn oil ⎤
1 teaspoon sesame oil ⎦ *combined*
oil for deep-frying
cucumber slices
tomato slices

Put chicken into a large bowl. Add coriander leaves, spring onions, garlic, ginger juice and remaining seasoning ingredients. Mix thoroughly and leave for at least 3 hours.

Lightly grease the inside of bags with combined corn oil and sesame oil. Put in chicken, fold and staple opening end.

Heat oil for deep-frying in a *kuali* and when hot put in packages and fry till chicken is cooked (approximately 15 minutes). Drain in a colander and serve hot garnished with cucumber and tomato slices.

Note: Ready-made Paper Chicken bags are available in Chinese sundry shops and supermarkets.

Chicken Wing Drumsticks

Preparation: 30 minutes   Cooking: 12 minutes   Makes: 24

12 chicken wings

Seasoning Ingredients
1 tablespoon ginger juice
1 teaspoon rice wine
1 teaspoon sugar
1 teaspoon salt
½ teaspoon monosodium glutamate
¼ teaspoon five-spice powder

Batter
3 tablespoons rice flour
3 tablespoons flour
1 teaspoon baking powder
¼ teaspoon salt
¼ teaspoon monosodium glutamate
pinch of five-spice powder
8 tablespoons water, or enough
   to mix batter to a runny
   consistency

oil for deep-frying

Chilli Sauce
12 red chillies
3 cloves garlic
2½ cm (1 in) ginger
2 tablespoons oyster sauce   *combined*
**1 tablespoon tomato sauce*   *and boiled*
½ tablespoon vinegar
1 teaspoon sugar
1 tablespoon oil

cucumber slices
tomato slices
pineapple slices

Cut off the tips of wings, then cut the wings into two at the joints.

Push meat to one end of each wing with the fingers and turn the skin inside out to form a chicken drumstick. Marinate drumsticks with seasoning ingredients and leave for 1 hour.

Combine batter ingredients in a mixing bowl.

Heat oil for deep-frying in a *kuali*. Dip drumsticks in batter and fry till light golden brown.

Serve hot with chilli sauce as a dip and, if desired, garnished with cucumber, tomato and pineapple slices.

Diced Chicken with Cashew Nuts

Preparation: 20 minutes   Cooking: 10 minutes

**1 whole chicken breastmeat, cut into
 1¼ cm (½ in) cubes**

Seasoning Ingredients
1 teaspoon sugar
1 teaspoon sesame oil
1 teaspoon salt
1 teaspoon rice wine
½ teaspoon monosodium glutamate
1 teaspoon cornflour
½ tablespoon corn oil

1 tablespoon corn oil
**6 dried Chinese mushrooms, soaked
 and diced**
3 tablespoons corn oil
1 onion, diced
1 can (425 g/15 oz) young corn, diced
2 green peppers, diced
1 medium carrot, diced and parboiled
90 g (3 oz) roasted cashew nuts

Sauce Ingredients
1 cup fresh chicken stock
2 dessertspoons oyster sauce
1 teaspoon light soy sauce
1 teaspoon sesame oil
1 teaspoon rice wine
½ teaspoon sugar
½ teaspoon salt
½ teaspoon monosodium glutamate
1 tablespoon cornflour

2 sprigs coriander leaves

Marinate chicken cubes with seasoning ingredients for at least 30 minutes.

Heat 1 tablespoon corn oil in a *kuali* and stir-fry mushrooms for a minute. Dish out and stir-fry marinated chicken until cooked. Remove and wash *kuali*.

Heat 3 tablespoons corn oil in the clean *kuali*. Fry onion until transparent and fragrant. Put in fried chicken, mushrooms and young corn and stir-fry for 1-2 minutes. Add green peppers, carrot and lastly cashew nuts. Stir in sauce ingredients.

Dish out and serve hot, garnished with coriander leaves.

Fried Lemon Chicken

Preparation: 10 minutes   Cooking: 15 minutes

1½ kg (3⅓ lb) chicken, cut into 2½ cm
   (1 in) pieces
2 dessertspoons light soy sauce
2 teaspoons sesame oil
½ teaspoon pepper
3 teaspoons salt
4 tablespoons cornflour
oil for deep-frying
2 tablespoons oil
3 tablespoons plum sauce } combined
2 tablespoons water
4 dessertspoons sugar
3 tablespoons lemon or } combined
   lime juice
3 sprigs coriander leaves

Marinate chicken with soy sauce, sesame oil, pepper and salt and leave for 30 minutes. Just before frying chicken mix in cornflour.

Heat oil for deep-frying in a *kuali* until hot. Lower heat, then fry marinated chicken, stirring frequently, for 10 minutes until golden brown. Remove with a perforated ladle and drain.

Heat 2 tablespoons oil in a *kuali*. Put in fried chicken and combined plum sauce and water and stir-fry for 1 minute. Add combined sugar and lemon or lime juice and stir-fry briskly.

Serve hot garnished with coriander leaves.

Green Stems with Crabmeat

Preparation: 20 minutes   Cooking: 10 minutes

1 kg (2⅕ lb) green stems ('kai choy')
1 teaspoon bicarbonate of soda
2 tablespoons oil
5 cloves garlic, minced
6 large button mushrooms, sliced

Sauce
2 cups fresh chicken stock
1 teaspoon salt
½ teaspoon sugar
½ teaspoon monosodium glutamate
½ teaspoon sesame oil
¼ teaspoon pepper
1 tablespoon cornflour

600 g (1⅓ lb) crabs, steamed, meat
   extracted
1 egg, beaten lightly

Trim green stems, discarding leafy parts, and cut into 7½ cm (3 in) lengths.

Boil half a *kuali* of water and stir in bicarbonate of soda and 1 teaspoon oil. Put in green stems and boil for 3-4 minutes. Remove and immerse in a basin of cold water. Rinse and drain.

Heat remaining oil in a *kuali* and lightly brown garlic. Put in mushrooms then green stems and stir-fry briskly for 1 minute. Pour in combined sauce ingredients and bring to a boil. Add crabmeat and when sauce thickens, gradually stir in beaten egg.

Place in a serving dish and serve immediately.

Fried Yam Rings with Mixed Vegetables

(photograph opposite)

Preparation: 10 minutes   Steaming: 25-30 minutes   Cooking: 8 minutes

1 kg (2¹/₅ lb) yam, peeled and cut
   into cubes (there should be 760 g/1³/₄ lb
   clean weight)
1½ teaspoons salt
1 teaspoon monosodium glutamate
1 teaspoon five-spice powder
2 dessertspoons sugar
1 tablespoon oil
60 g (2 oz) wheat starch flour
   ('tang meen fun')
oil for deep-frying
1 small head lettuce

Filling
see recipe for Diced Chicken with Cashew
   Nuts (page 76)

Place yam cubes in a steamer and steam for 25-30 minutes until soft.

Mash yam cubes while still hot until free from lumps. Add salt, monosodium glutamate, five-spice powder, sugar and oil. When well combined, add wheat starch flour and knead well.

Divide yam dough into two equal portions. Lightly flour board and hands with wheat starch flour and form into two 15 cm (6 in) diameter hollow rings.

Place yam rings on a flat colander for deep-frying.

Heat oil for deep-frying in a *kuali* until hot. Lower heat to medium and deep-fry yam rings, one at a time, for approximately 4 minutes until golden in colour.

Remove and place on a dish garnished with lettuce. Fill yam rings with diced chicken and mixed vegetables and serve immediately.

Note: Choose a good powdery yam for this recipe.

Opposite: Fried Yam Rings with Mixed Vegetables

Fried Turnip and Cloud Ear Fungus

Preparation: 15 minutes   Cooking: 10 minutes

240 g (8 oz) chicken or pork, cut into strips

Seasoning Ingredients
2 teaspoons light soy sauce
½ teaspoon sesame oil
½ teaspoon salt
½ teaspoon pepper
½ teaspoon sugar
½ teaspoon monosodium glutamate
2 teaspoons cornflour

3 tablespoons oil
3 cloves garlic
240 g (8 oz) turnip, cut into strips
**4 cloud ear fungus, soaked and cut
   into thin strips**

Sauce
1 cup fresh chicken stock
1 teaspoon dark soy sauce
1 teaspoon sesame oil
2 teaspoons light soy sauce
1 teaspoon sugar
1 teaspoon salt
¼ teaspoon pepper

3 teaspoons cornflour ⎱ *combined*
1 tablespoon water ⎰

1 stalk spring onion ⎱ *cut into 5 cm*
2 sprigs coriander leaves ⎰ *(2 in) lengths*

Marinate chicken or pork strips with seasoning ingredients and leave for 30 minutes.

Heat 1 tablespoon of the oil in a *kuali* and brown garlic. Add meat and fry over high heat for 1 minute. Dish out and leave aside.

Wash *kuali* and heat remaining oil until hot. Put in turnip, stir-fry and cover *kuali* for 1 minute. Remove cover, add cloud ear fungus and stir-fry quickly. Add sauce ingredients and bring to a boil. Put in fried meat then stir in thickening.

Serve hot, garnished with spring onion and coriander leaves.

Fried Soybean Cake with Chilli

(photograph on page 56)

Preparation: 15 minutes Cooking: 8 minutes

2 soft soybean cakes
90 g (3 oz) chicken or pork, minced

Seasoning Ingredients
½ teaspoon light soy sauce
½ teaspoon salt
¼ teaspoon sesame oil
pinch of pepper
pinch of monosodium glutamate

3 tablespoons oil
4 cloves garlic ⎫
3 red chillies, seeded ⎬ *minced*
2 teaspoons preserved soy beans,
**   minced separately**
1 stalk leek, sliced at a slant

Sauce
½ cup fresh chicken stock or water
1 teaspoon oyster sauce
½ teaspoon sugar
½ teaspoon sesame oil
½ teaspoon salt
½ teaspoon dark soy sauce
¼ teaspoon pepper
2 teaspoons cornflour

2 stalks spring onion, chopped

Cut soybean cakes into 4 cm (1½ in) pieces.

Season meat with seasoning ingredients and leave for 15 minutes.

Heat oil in a *kuali* and fry garlic and chillies until fragrant. Add preserved soy beans and fry till aromatic.

Put in minced meat, then leek and stir-fry for half a minute. Add soybean cakes, stir-fry for 2 minutes, breaking soybean cakes gently with frying spatula. Pour in prepared sauce ingredients and boil until gravy thickens. Add spring onions, dish out and serve hot with rice.

Fried Hokkien Mee, KL Style

Preparation: 20 minutes   Cooking: 12 minutes

150 g (5 oz) small prawns, shelled
5 small cuttlefish, cut into rings
½ teaspoon sesame oil
¼ teaspoon pepper
½ tablespoon light soy sauce
2 tablespoons oil
3 shallots, sliced
120 g (4 oz) chicken fat or
    pork fat, diced
4 cloves garlic, minced
6 slices fish cake
3-4 stalks mustard green, cut into
    5 cm (2 in) lengths
450 g (1 lb) fresh yellow noodles
2 cups water
1 tablespoon dark thick soy sauce
½ teaspoon monosodium glutamate
a few leaves lettuce, cut into strips

Sambal Belacan

5 x 5 x ½ cm (2 x 2 x ¼ in) dried
    shrimp paste
8 red chillies
3 small limes

Season prawns and cuttlefish with sesame oil, pepper and light soy sauce. Leave aside.

Heat oil in a *kuali* and brown shallots. Remove and put aside.

Reheat *kuali* and add chicken or pork fat. Fry until crisp. Remove fat crisps with a perforated ladle. Leave oil behind.

When *kuali* is smoking hot, add minced garlic, seasoned prawns, cuttlefish and fish cake slices. Add mustard greens, stir-fry for a few seconds. Put in noodles and fry for 2 minutes.

Add water, dark thick soy sauce and monosodium glutamate. Stir to combine sauce and cover *kuali* for 1 minute. Remove cover and add shallot crisps and fat crisps.

Serve hot, sprinkled with lettuce strips and accompanied with a small dish of Sambal Belacan.

Sambal Belacan

Roast dried shrimp paste in a clean pan over low heat till fragrant and, while hot, pound with red chillies until smooth. Put into a small dish and squeeze in lime juice.

Jemput Pisang

Preparation: 10 minutes   Cooking: 10 minutes   Makes: approximately 40

2 eggs
30 g (1 oz) sugar
¼ teaspoon salt
120 g (4 oz) self-raising flour ⎫
30 g (1 oz) cornflour   ⎬ *sifted together*
1 teaspoon baking powder   ⎭
½ coconut, grated (for ½ cup
    coconut milk)
5 medium bananas ('pisang rastali'),
    mashed
oil for deep-frying

Whisk eggs and sugar until light and fluffy. Add salt and fold in sifted ingredients alternately with coconut milk. Add mashed bananas and mix well.

Heat oil in a *kuali* and fry tablespoonfuls of batter until golden brown. Drain well before serving.

Kuih Bingka Special

Preparation: 20 minutes   Baking: 1 hour 20 minutes   Oven setting: 205°C, 400°F, Gas Regulo 8

4 cups grated young tapioca
450 g (1 lb) sugar
½ white coconut (approx. 240 g/8 oz),
    grated finely
½ coconut, grated (for 1¼ cups
    coconut milk)
60 g (2 oz) flour
2 eggs, beaten lightly (reserve a
    little for glazing)
60 g (2 oz) butter at room temperature
4 tablespoons evaporated milk
¼ teaspoon salt

Mix grated tapioca with remaining ingredients and mix thoroughly.

Pour into an ungreased 21½ cm (8½ in) square cake tin and bake in a hot oven for 1 hour and 20 minutes.

Brush surface with reserved beaten egg and bake for a further 3 minutes until top is firm and light golden.

Remove from oven and leave to cool thoroughly before cutting into 2 cm (¾ in) thick slices.

Note: If you have an electric chopper, cut tapioca into very small pieces, discarding the central fibre, and blend until fine.

Taufu Fah

(photograph opposite)

Preparation: 25 minutes   Cooking: 25 minutes   Makes: 12 servings

Taufu Fah
300 g (10 oz) soy beans
12 cups water
45 g (1½ oz) cornflour
1 teaspoon 'sekko' powder, sifted
½ cup hot water

Soybean Milk
reserved soybean pulp
6 cups water
200 g (6½ oz) sugar
4 screwpine leaves, knotted

Syrup
1¼ cups water
420 g (15 oz) sugar
2½ cm (1 in) ginger
3 screwpine leaves, knotted

Note: Sekko powder is available in Chinese medical shops. It is also sold in stone form. This has to be ground to a fine powder before use as the smoothness of Taufu Fah is largely dependent on powder-fine sekko.

Taufu Fah
Wash and soak soy beans for at least 5 hours, preferably overnight. Drain.

Blend soaked soy beans in an electric blender, half at a time, with 1½ cups of the water, until fine. Strain mixture over a fine piece of muslin cloth and squeeze pulp until dry. Add a little more water and squeeze again. (Reserve soybean pulp to make soybean milk.)

Strain concentrated soybean milk over a clean piece of muslin cloth again, this time into a large cooking pot. Add remaining water. Bring to a boil over moderate heat, stirring all the time with a wooden spoon. This will take approximately 15-20 minutes. Remove bubbles from the surface while stirring.

Before soybean milk comes to a boil, blend cornflour and *sekko* powder with ½ cup hot water until dissolved. Pour into a fairly large aluminium pot — a medium rice cooker pot will do nicely.

As soon as soybean milk comes to a boil, pour immediately, from a height of about ⅓ metre (1 foot) over cornflour mixture. Quickly remove surface bubbles with a ladle and cover pot with a towel. Place lid over the towel and leave undisturbed for at least 40 minutes to set before serving.

To serve, carefully scoop thin layers of Taufu Fah into individual small bowls. Add 1½-2 tablespoonfuls of syrup and serve either hot or cold.

Soybean Milk
Place reserved soybean pulp, water, sugar and screwpine leaves into a large pot and bring to a boil, stirring frequently. Allow to simmer for 5 minutes, then strain over a muslin cloth. When cool, refrigerate and serve as a drink.

Syrup
Put water, sugar, ginger and screwpine leaves in a small saucepan and bring to a boil, stirring until sugar dissolves. Remove and strain.

Opposite: Taufu Fah

Kuih Lapis

Preparation: 20 minutes   Cooking: 50 minutes

700 g (1½ lb) wet rice flour
105 g (3½ oz) tapioca flour
30 g (1 oz) green bean flour } *sifted*
1½ coconuts, grated (for 5½ cups
   coconut milk)

Syrup
600 g (1⅓ lb) sugar
1 cup water } *boiled and strained*
3 screwpine leaves, knotted

red colouring

Put rice flour, tapioca flour and green bean flour in a bowl. Gradually pour in coconut milk and mix to a smooth batter.

Pour syrup gradually into the flour mixture, stirring all the time until it is well blended.

Divide the flour mixture into two portions. Leave one portion uncoloured and add a few drops of red colouring to the other, blending well.

Place a 25-27 cm (10-11 in) round deep tray in a steamer over rapidly boiling water. Pour 1 cup of white batter into the pan and steam over moderate heat for 4 minutes. Remove cover, wipe the underlid with a dry towel, then pour 1 cup of pink batter over the cooked white layer. Steam for 4 minutes. Repeat, alternating white and pink layers until all the batter is used up.

For the final layer add another 1 or 2 drops of red colouring to pink batter to give a stronger-coloured layer. Remove cake to cool thoroughly for at least 6-7 hours before cutting.

Note: Use a plastic knife or spatula to cut Kuih Lapis. The spatula supplied with an electric mixer will do beautifully.

Serimuka Keledek

Preparation: 20 minutes   Cooking: 1 hour

700 g (1½ lb) sweet potatoes (yellow variety), steamed, peeled and mashed
180 g (6 oz) tapioca flour, sifted
1 coconut, grated (for 1³/₄ cups thick coconut milk to be reserved for topping, and 1 cup thin coconut milk)
3 teaspoons salt
3-4 drops yellow colouring

Topping
3 large eggs
180 g (6 oz) sugar
1³/₄ cups reserved thick coconut milk
45 g (1½ oz) tapioca flour, sifted
¼ teaspoon salt
1 tablespoon screwpine juice (obtained by blending 6-7 screwpine leaves with a little water)
2-3 drops green colouring

Combine well-mashed sweet potatoes with sifted tapioca flour, thin coconut milk, salt and yellow colouring. Mix well. Put in a 25-27 cm (10-11 in) round pan and steam for 20 minutes until cooked.

Pour prepared topping over steamed sweet potato layer and steam again for 25 minutes over medium heat. Cool thoroughly before cutting.

Topping
Stir eggs and sugar together in a bowl. Do not beat. Mix in thick coconut milk, sifted tapioca flour and salt. Lastly stir in screwpine juice and green colouring. Strain to remove lumps.

PAHANG

Pahang State is the largest in Peninsular Malaysia and within its borders are the famous hill resorts of Cameron Highlands, Fraser's Hill and Genting Highlands. Like Kelantan and Trengganu, there are stretches of fine beaches dotted with picturesque fishing villages, unhurried and leisurely. Kuantan, its bustling capital, has rapidly developed into a popular holiday resort with modern amenities.

Malaysia's longest river, the Sungei Pahang, and its tributaries are teeming with freshwater fish like the *ikan jelawat, ikan kelah* and *ikan kerai.*

They are in high demand and are highly priced. Thick tropical jungle covers large tracts of Pahang. Predominantly rural, like the States of Kelantan and Trengganu, typical east coast cottage industries like silverware crafting, silk weaving and batik printing flourish here.

Malay food with the east coast flavour is relatively simple to prepare and the locals use mild spices enlivened with chillies and fragrant roots.

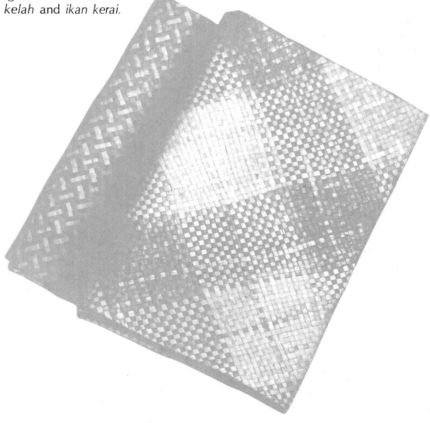

Opposite: Puding Raja

Gulai Ikan

Preparation: 15 minutes   Cooking: 15 minutes

2 thick slices spanish mackerel
1 teaspoon salt
1 teaspoon pepper
1 coconut, grated (for 1 cup thick coconut milk and 1 cup thin coconut milk)

Ground Ingredients
10 bird chillies
2½ cm (1 in) turmeric root
2 slices galingale
1 stalk lemon grass, sliced

2 pieces dried tamarind skin
1 teaspoon salt

Season fish with salt and pepper.

Mix thin coconut milk with ground ingredients and tamarind skin in a pot and bring to a slow boil. Add fish and thick coconut milk and stir carefully till gravy thickens and fish is tender. Add salt to taste.

Gulai Botok

Preparation: 20 minutes   Cooking: 30 minutes

2 slices (9 cm/3½ in thick) spanish mackerel
2 teaspoons salt
6 pieces dried tamarind skin
30 bird chillies ⎱ *ground finely*
2½ cm (1 in) turmeric root ⎰
1 coconut, grated (for 3 cups coconut milk)
60 g (2 oz) 'terung pipit'
3 'terung asam' or 3 pieces dried tamarind skin
½ teaspoon salt

Rub fish with salt and tamarind skin and leave overnight in the refrigerator. Next day, put fish in a saucepan of boiling water and boil until fish is cooked. Flake fish and lightly mash with a spoon.

Mix fish with ground ingredients, coconut milk, *terung pipit* and *terung asam* and cook over low heat, stirring frequently, for 15-20 minutes until oil appears on surface. Add salt to taste.

Note: Terung pipit grows wild. It is green in colour and the size of green peas with lots of tiny seeds. When cooked, it tastes like eggplant. It is known as terung rembang in some other States, for example in Negri Sembilan and Perak. Terung asam is yellow in colour and is very sour. If not available, use tamarind skin as a substitute.

Masak Tempoyak Ikan Jelawat

Preparation: 15 minutes   Cooking: 15 minutes

**1 sultan fish ('ikan jelawat', 'ikan kelah' or
 'ikan kerai')**
1 teaspoon salt
4 pieces dried tamarind skin

Ground Ingredients
2 tablespoons fermented durian
10 bird chillies
6 mm (¼ in) turmeric root
5 sprigs polygonum leaves

1 teaspoon salt
4 cups water

Rub fish with salt and tamarind skin and leave aside for 15 minutes, then wash fish and put in a pot together with ground ingredients and salt. Add water and bring to a boil.

Cook over low heat for 10 minutes until fish is cooked, taking care not to overcook fish. Serve hot with rice.

Note: Ikan jelawat, ikan kelah and ikan kerai are freshwater river fish. Ikan kelah is the most sought-after fish with soft scales and is usually cooked without removing the scales.

Rendang Daging

Preparation: 20 minutes   Cooking: 1½ hours

**600 g (1⅓ lb) beef, cut into 2½ cm
 (1 in) pieces**
1 teaspoon black peppercorns, ground
1 teaspoon salt
**1½ coconuts, grated (for 5 cups
 coconut milk)**

Ground Ingredients
15 dried chillies, soaked
15 bird chillies
2½ cm (1 in) galingale
2½ cm (1 in) turmeric root
2½ cm (1 in) ginger
15 shallots
5 cloves garlic

1 piece dried tamarind skin
2 stalks lemon grass, crushed lightly
2 turmeric leaves
1½ teaspoons salt

Season meat with black pepper and salt and leave for 30 minutes. In a pot, mix coconut milk and ground ingredients and bring to a slow boil.

Add meat, dried tamarind skin, lemon grass and turmeric leaves. Simmer gently for 1¼ -1½ hours until meat is tender and gravy becomes thick and oily. Add salt to taste and discard lemon grass and turmeric leaves.

Pincuk Daging

Preparation: 15 minutes   Cooking: 1 hour

600 g (1⅓ lb) beef
1 coconut, grated (for 'pati santan')
½ white coconut, grated for 'kerisik'
10 shallots, sliced
2 teaspoons black peppercorns, ground
     finely
1 teaspoon salt
juice of 1 big lime

Put beef in a saucepan of water and boil until tender. Remove and cut into 5 cm (2 in) square slices.

Combine sliced beef with *pati santan, kerisik,* shallots, black pepper, salt and lime juice and mix well. Serve with rice.

Note: Pincuk Daging is usually served in kenduris.

Ayam Golek, Pahang Style

Preparation: 15 minutes   Cooking: 20 minutes   Grilling: 50-60 minutes

1½ kg (3⅓ lb) chicken, halved, with a few
     slits made on back and thighs
2 teaspoons salt
1 teaspoon turmeric powder or 2½ cm
     (1 in) turmeric root, ground

Ground Ingredients
25 dried chillies, soaked
300 g (10 oz) shallots
2 stalks lemon grass
1¼ cm (½ in) ginger

1½ tablespoons chicken curry powder
1 tablespoon sugar
1 teaspoon salt
½ teaspoon monosodium glutamate
2 small pieces dried tamarind skin
1 coconut, grated (for 2 cups coconut
     milk)
lettuce, cucumbers,
     tomatoes or chillies
     for garnishing

Rub chicken with salt and turmeric powder and leave for 15 minutes.

Mix ground ingredients, curry powder, sugar, salt, monosodium glutamate, dried tamarind skin and coconut milk in a saucepan and bring to a slow boil, stirring over low heat for approximately 20 minutes until gravy is thick.

Grill chicken over glowing charcoal for 15-20 minutes on each side until chicken is browned and cooked. Spoon gravy over chicken and grill again for 5 minutes until fragrant and oily. Place on a dish and serve, if desired, garnished with lettuce, cucumber, tomatoes and chillies.

Note: Mackerel (ikan kembong) or black pomfret (ikan bawal hitam) can be grilled this way. Use 1½ tablespoons fish curry powder instead of chicken curry powder.

Gulai Maman

Preparation: 15 minutes   Cooking: 20 minutes

2 bunches 'maman' vegetables
1 teaspoon salt
2 thick slices spanish mackerel
1½ teaspoons salt
12 bird chillies ⎫
1¼ cm (½ in) turmeric root ⎬ *ground*
3 pieces dried tamarind skin ⎭
½ teaspoon monosodium glutamate
1 coconut, grated (for 4 cups coconut
   milk)

Wash *maman* and mix with salt. Lightly squeeze out the juice, then rinse thoroughly with water.

Put half the vegetable in a pot and on top of this add fish, salt, ground ingredients, tamarind skin and monosodium glutamate. Place remaining vegetables on top and carefully pour in coconut milk to cover ingredients.

Cook over low heat without stirring until gravy is thick.

Note: Maman vegetable is clover shaped and the size of red spinach. It is usually grown in the padi fields of Pahang before a new crop of padi is planted.

Masak Acar Taucu

Preparation: 15 minutes   Cooking: 12 minutes

2 medium cucumbers
3 tablespoons oil
5 shallots ⎫
2 cloves garlic ⎬ *sliced*
1¼ cm (½ in) ginger, chopped
45 g (1½ oz) dried anchovies,
   heads and entrails
   removed, chopped
3 dessertspoons preserved soy beans,
   ground coarsely
1 tablespoon tamarind paste ⎫ *mixed and*
1½ cups water ⎬ *strained*
2 onions, each slit across the top to form a
   flower (see diagram, page 106)
10 green chillies, split lengthwise without
   cutting through
pinch of salt (if desired)

Cut cucumber into four lengthwise and remove seed portions. Cut into 4 cm (1½ in) strips. Make two slits in the centre of each strip without cutting through cucumber.

Heat oil in *kuali* and lightly brown shallots, garlic, ginger and dried anchovies. Add preserved soy beans and fry until fragrant. Put in tamarind juice and bring to a slow boil. Add onions and cucumbers and lastly green chillies. Simmer for a few minutes, taking care not to overcook cucumbers. If necessary, add a pinch of salt.

Note: Masak Acar Taucu is very often served in kenduris.

Laksa Pahang

Preparation: 30 minutes Cooking: 40 minutes   Serves: 8-10

8 medium to large mackerels
2 teaspoons salt
2 screwpine leaves, knotted
1¼ cups oil

Ground Ingredients
30 dried chillies, soaked
15 shallots
2 stalks lemon grass
2½ cm (1 in) galingale
1¼ cm (½ in) ginger
1 teaspoon turmeric powder
1½ tablespoons fish curry powder

120 g (4 oz) white grated coconut for
   'kerisik' ground separately
1 coconut, grated (for 8 cups coconut
   milk)
2 pieces dried tamarind skin
2 teaspoons salt
1 teaspoon sugar
1 teaspoon monosodium glutamate
1 packet (600 g/1⅓ lb) thick rice
   vermicelli, scalded and drained

Garnishing Ingredients
1 cucumber, shredded
6-8 long beans, uncooked, chopped
300 g (10 oz) beansprouts, tailed
2 onions, shredded
2 turmeric leaves ⎫
1 small bunch basil leaves ⎭ *sliced finely*

Side Dish
8-10 red chillies, ground separately
5 x 1¼ cm (2 x ½ in) dried shrimp paste,
   toasted and ground separately
salt

Rub fish with salt and cook in half a saucepan of boiling water together with screwpine leaves. Flake and grind or blend fish till fine.

Heat oil and fry ground ingredients and *kerisik* until fragrant and oil appears on surface. Add ground fish, coconut milk, tamarind skin, salt, sugar and monosodium glutamate and bring to a slow boil. Lower heat and simmer for 20 minutes, stirring frequently.

To serve, put a little thick rice vermicelli into individual serving dishes and garnish with a little of each garnishing ingredient. Pour hot fish gravy over and serve hot with a side dish of ground chillies, dried shrimp paste and salt.

Dadar

Preparation: 20 minutes Cooking: 50 minutes Makes: 18 pancakes

Pancakes
300 g (10 oz) flour
2 egg yolks, beaten lightly
½ teaspoon salt
1 coconut, grated (for 3½ cups coconut milk)
½ teaspoon vanilla essence
a few drops green colouring

Coconut Milk Sauce
1 white coconut, grated (for 2 cups coconut milk)
150 g (5 oz) sugar
2 egg yolks, beaten lightly
¼ teaspoon salt
3 screwpine leaves, knotted
    or

Durian Sauce
flesh from 1 medium durian (do not remove seeds if desired)
1 coconut, grated (for 5 cups coconut milk)
120 g (4 oz) brown sugar
pinch of salt
4 screwpine leaves, knotted

Pancakes
Sift flour into a mixing bowl. Add lightly beaten egg yolks, salt and gradually blend in coconut milk. Stir in vanilla essence and green colouring. Strain to remove lumps.

Grease and heat a 15-18 cm (6-7 in) pan with oil. Pour a ladleful (about 4 tablespoons) batter into the pan to form a thin layer. Cook over very low heat for 1-2 minutes. Place on a dish and repeat with remaining batter.

Arrange pancakes in two neat stacks. Serve cut in wedges and top with Coconut Milk Sauce or Durian Sauce.

Coconut Milk Sauce
Combine all ingredients in a saucepan and stir continuously over low heat with a flat wooden spoon for approximately 15 minutes until sauce thickens.

Durian Sauce
Combine all ingredients and stir over moderate heat until sauce thickens. If keeping the seeds, remember durian seeds are edible. Allow sauce to simmer, stirring occasionally, until seeds are cooked.

Puding Raja

(photograph on page 88)

Preparation: 10 minutes   Cooking: 15 minutes

oil for deep-frying
2 combs or approx. 24 bananas ('pisang
   lemak manis'/'pisang susu'), peeled
5 red cherries, sliced

Jala Emas
240 g (8 oz) sugar
1 cup water
2 screwpine leaves, knotted
6 duck's egg yolks
1 egg yolk   } *beaten lightly*
½ teaspoon rose essence

Sauce
1 can (410 g/15 oz) evaporated milk
2 dessertspoons condensed milk
1 egg, beaten lightly
½ cup water
¼ teaspoon rose or vanilla essence

Heat oil in a *kuali* and deep-fry bananas, a few at a time, over low heat for 5 minutes or until golden in colour. Drain on absorbent paper and arrange in a serving dish. Top with prepared Jala Emas. Decorate with cherries and serve with chilled sauce.

Jala Emas
Put sugar, water and screwpine leaves in a saucepan and bring to a slow boil, stirring until sugar dissolves. Remove screwpine leaves.

Put a ladleful of beaten yolks into a fine tea strainer and drizzle over boiling syrup, using a circular motion. When network of egg is cooked, stir carefully with a small ladle to give it an even coating of syrup. Remove with a perforated ladle and place on a serving dish. Lightly separate Jala Emas with a chopstick or fork.

Sauce
Put evaporated milk, condensed milk, lightly beaten egg, water and essence in a saucepan and bring to a slow boil, stirring continuously. Remove from heat and strain into a serving jug. Chill in a refrigerator.

Note: Bananas should not be too ripe, otherwise they will not keep their shape after frying. Pisang lemak manis/pisang susu are slightly larger and firmer than pisang emas. Puding Raja and Ayam Golek (page 92) are very popular traditional dishes for royal weddings and royal festive celebrations in Pahang.

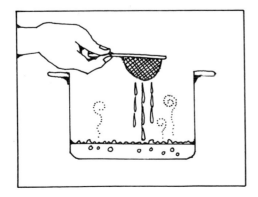

Hati Pari

Preparation: 15 minutes   Cooking: 40 minutes

Topping/Minyak Muda
1 coconut, grated (for 1 cup 'pati santan')
pinch of salt

Kuih
300 g (10 oz) rice flour
120 g (4 oz) palm sugar, chopped
120 g (4 oz) sugar
½ cup water
2 screwpine leaves, knotted
1½ coconuts, grated (for 5 cups
   coconut milk)

Topping
Put *pati santan* with salt into a *kuali* and stir over low heat with a wooden spatula for 30 minutes. Oil will separate from coconut residue. Continue stirring until coconut residue turns a rich brown. Remove from heat and drain.

Kuih
Sift rice flour into a mixing bowl. Put palm sugar and sugar in water with screwpine leaves. Melt sugar over low heat, stirring frequently. Strain syrup.

Stir syrup and coconut milk into rice flour and blend until smooth. Strain mixture into a cooking pot and cook over low heat until mixture forms a lump of cooked dough.

Put mixture into an 18 x 27 cm (7 x 11 in) shallow tin and smoothen surface while it is still hot with a piece of banana leaf. Sprinkle with prepared coconut residue crisps. Leave to cool thoroughly before cutting.

PERAK

Perak, the 'Silver State', has a multiracial population which ensures a wide range of cuisines. Truly outstanding specialties are the Malay curry dishes, especially the rendangs and Gulai Tempoyak. Methods of preparation are as exotic as the names. Rendang Tok with slices of young coconut is *lemak* and extremely rich; both Rendang Terlagi-lagi and Rendang Dinding are redolent in thick black sauce and irresistibly delicious; good and spicy Daging Masak Pesamah and Rendang Ayam Pedas are all-time favourites; and although Gulai Tempoyak (fermented salted durian) has a slightly unusual smell to the uninitiated, it is nevertheless appetising.

Ipoh, the state capital, is a municipality full of bustle and local character. The specialty here is *sar ho fun* (flat rice noodles) which is unrivalled for smoothness and soft texture. Apparently, this is due to the hardness of the water in the Perak region, but it must be partly attributable to the quality of the rice flour used, and to the skill of the maker. Whatever the reason, it remains a well-guarded secret.

Equally famous and just as unique as the Ipoh limestone caves are the Ipoh beansprouts. Fat, crisp and almost tailless, they are indeed 'king' of all beansprouts. This too has been attributed to the underground water of the Ipoh region, especially the Buntong area.

Opposite: Rendang Tok and Nasi Himpit

Ikan Asam Rebus with Pineapple

Preparation: 10 minutes   Cooking: 25 minutes

450 g (1 lb) spanish mackerel, sliced
1 teaspoon salt

Ground Ingredients
8 red chillies, seeded
8 bird chillies
2 stalks lemon grass
1¼ cm (½ in) turmeric root
10 shallots

2½ cups water
2 pieces dried tamarind skin
½ pineapple, sliced
1 teaspoon sugar
1 teaspoon salt

Clean fish and rub with salt.

Blend ground ingredients with water and bring to a slow boil. Add dried tamarind skin and allow to boil over low heat for 10 minutes. Put in pineapple slices and continue simmering for a further 5 minutes. Add fish, sugar and salt and cook for 5 minutes.

Serve hot with white rice.

Ikan Terubuk Masak Asam Tempoyak

Preparation: 10 minutes   Cooking: 15 minutes

2 slices shad or red snapper
1 teaspoon salt
3 tablespoons fermented durian
2 cups water
1¼ cm (½ in) turmeric root, ground finely
4-5 red chillies
1 onion } *ground coarsely*
30 g (1 oz) dried anchovies
1 stalk lemon grass, crushed lightly
1 turmeric leaf
1 teaspoon sugar
½ teaspoon salt
450 g (1 lb) soybean sprouts, tailed

Wash fish and rub with salt.

Mix fermented durian with water, turmeric, coarsely ground ingredients, lemon grass, turmeric leaf, sugar and salt and bring to a slow boil. Lower heat and simmer for 10 minutes then add fish and soybean sprouts and simmer till cooked. Discard turmeric leaf.

Note: To ferment durian, scrape durian flesh from the seeds. Mix with salt and leave in an airtight jar in the refrigerator for at least 3 days before use. Tempoyak can be kept refrigerated for months. Tempoyak is also commonly served as a sambal taken with rice. To serve Sambal Tempoyak, pound 4-5 chillies coarsely with a pinch of salt. Mix with 2 tablespoons of tempoyak or serve separately.

Pindang Udang

Preparation: 25 minutes   Cooking: 10 minutes

600 g (1⅓ lb) medium prawns
1 teaspoon salt
4 tablespoons oil
7 shallots, sliced
8 stalks lemon grass, sliced very fine
3 red chillies, sliced at a slant
2½ cm (1 in) turmeric root, ground
4-5 small sour starfruit, halved lengthwise
½ coconut, grated (for 1 cup coconut milk)
½ teaspoon salt

Shell prawns, leaving tails behind. Devein the prawns and rub with salt.

Heat oil in a *kuali* and fry shallots, lemon grass, red chillies, and ground turmeric. Put in prawns and stir-fry continuously. Add small sour starfruit and coconut milk and bring to a slow boil. Simmer for 1-2 minutes and stir in salt to taste.

Rendang Tok

(photograph on page 98)

Preparation: 20 minutes   Cooking: 2-2½ hours

1½ kg (3⅓ lb) beef, cut into 5 cm (2 in) cubes
150 g (5 oz) shallots ⎫ *sliced*
120 g (4 oz) garlic ⎭
150 g (5 oz) ginger, shredded

Ground Ingredients
2 heaped tablespoons coriander powder
2 tablespoons chilli powder
1 teaspoon cummin
1 teaspoon fennel
½ teaspoon black peppercorns
10 cardamoms
10 cloves
5 cm (2 in) stick cinnamon
1 teaspoon turmeric powder

½ white coconut, grated for 'kerisik'
½ young but firm white coconut, brown skin removed, cut into thin 5 cm (2 in) slices
5 coconuts, grated (for 'pati santan')
3 teaspoons salt

Marinate beef with sliced, shredded and ground ingredients, *kerisik*, sliced coconut and *pati santan*. Leave for 2 hours.

Put marinated ingredients in a pot and bring to a slow boil. Simmer over low heat, stirring frequently, for 2-2½ hours until meat is tender and almost black in colour and dry. To prevent meat and gravy from sticking to pan, stir continuously when gravy is almost dry. Add salt to taste.

Note: Rendang Tok is popularly served in kenduris as well as during festive celebrations with nasi himpit (compressed rice cakes). It keeps well in the refrigerator for at least a week.

Rendang Dinding

Preparation: 20 minutes   Cooking: 1 ¼ hours

1 kg (2¹/₅ lb) beef, cut into 6 mm (¼ in)
   thick slices
1 cup oil
1 kg (2¹/₅ lb) onions, sliced
3 cloves garlic, sliced
5 cm (2 in) ginger, shredded
3 tablespoons oil
45 dried chillies, soaked }
5 cloves garlic   } *ground*
1 dessertspoon dark thick soy sauce
2 tablespoons tamarind paste } *mixed and*
3 cups water   } *strained*
2 tablespoons brown sugar
2 heaped teaspoons salt
1 teaspoon monosodium glutamate

Cut meat across the grain into 6 mm (¼ in) thick slices and score slices lightly.

Heat 1 cup oil in a *kuali* and fry sliced onions, garlic and ginger for 5-7 minutes. Drain off oil and grind fried ingredients coarsely. Leave aside.

Add 3 tablespoons oil to *kuali* and fry ground chillies and garlic till oil separates. Put in meat, then the coarsely ground fried ingredients and soy sauce. Continue frying for 15 minutes.

Pour in tamarind juice, add brown sugar, salt and monosodium glutamate and stir frequently over low heat until gravy is thick and meat tender. Serve with boiled white rice or Roti Jala (page 160).

Rendang Terlagi-lagi

Preparation: 20 minutes   Cooking: 1 hour

1 cup oil
600 g (1 ⅓ lb) beef, cut into 4 cm (1 ½ in)
   slices, 6 mm (¼ in) thick
1 tablespoon dark thick soy sauce
20 dried chillies, soaked and ground
   separately
300 g (10 oz) shallots }
4 cloves garlic   } *ground*
2½ cm (1 in) ginger }
4 stalks lemon grass, crushed
1½ coconuts, grated (for 'pati santan')
1 tablespoon tamarind paste } *mixed and*
5 tablespoons water   } *strained*
½ white coconut, grated for 'kerisik'
1 teaspoon sugar
½ teaspoon monosodium glutamate
1½ teaspoons salt

Heat oil in a *kuali* and fry beef slices over moderate heat for 15 minutes. Drain from oil and lightly pound meat while still hot. Season cooked meat with dark thick soy sauce and leave for 1 hour.

Reheat *kuali* and fry ground chillies for 2-3 minutes, then add ground ingredients and crushed lemon grass. Fry until fragrant and oil separates.

Put in seasoned beef and mix well. Add *pati santan* and tamarind juice and bring to a boil. Lower heat, simmer until almost dry, then add *kerisik*, sugar, monosodium glutamate and salt to taste. Stir continuously until gravy is very thick.

Note: When you have tasted this Rendang you will ask for more, hence the name Rendang Terlagi-lagi. Try it, you'll not be disappointed.

Rendang Daging Perak

Preparation: 20 minutes Cooking: 1³/₄ hours

1 kg (2¹/₅ lb) beef, cut into 2½ cm (1 in)
  cubes
1 teaspoon salt
1 cup oil
2½ cm (1 in) galingale, crushed
2 stalks lemon grass, crushed

Ground Ingredients
20 dried chillies, soaked and ground
  separately
2½ cm (1 in) galingale
2½ cm (1 in) ginger
2½ cm (1 in) turmeric root
3 stalks lemon grass
600 g (1¹/₃ lb) shallots
1 whole pod garlic

2 coconuts, grated (for 5 cups coconut
  milk)
3 turmeric leaves, 2 of them cut finely
2 teaspoons salt

Season meat with salt and leave aside for 15 minutes.

Heat oil in a *kuali* and fry crushed galingale and lemon grass. Fry ground chillies, then add other ground ingredients and fry, stirring constantly over low heat, till fragrant and oil separates.

Put in meat and stir-fry until water evaporates. Add coconut milk and the whole turmeric leaf and bring slowly to a boil, stirring constantly. Reduce heat further and cook for approximately 1½ hours, stirring frequently. Remove turmeric leaf and when meat is tender and gravy becomes thick and oily, add finely sliced turmeric leaves and salt to taste. Remove from heat.

Daging Masak Pesamah

Preparation: 20 minutes Cooking: 1½ hours

600 g (1¹/₃ lb) beef
³/₄ cup oil
5 shallots, sliced
5 cm (2 in) stick cinnamon
2 cardamoms
4 cloves
2 sections of a star anise
10 shallots
4 cloves garlic   } ground
2½ cm (1 in) ginger
10 tablespoons meat curry powder
½ white coconut, grated for 'kerisik'
1 tablespoon tamarind paste | *mixed and*
1 cup water | *strained*
1 coconut, grated (for 4 cups coconut
  milk)
1 teaspoon sugar
2 teaspoons salt

Cut beef into thin slices across the grain.

Heat oil in a pot and fry shallots for 2 minutes, then spices until fragrant. Add ground ingredients and fry for a few minutes.

Combine curry powder, *kerisik* and tamarind juice into a paste. If necessary, add a little extra water. Fry over moderate heat until fragrant and oil separates. It may be necessary to add a little of the coconut milk to prevent ground ingredients from sticking to pan.

Put in beef and a cup of coconut milk. Stir-fry rapidly to mix ingredients. Pour in remaining coconut milk, add sugar and salt and simmer over low heat, stirring frequently, until meat is tender and gravy is thick and almost dry.

Ayam Panggang

(photograph opposite)

Preparation: 20 minutes   Cooking: 10 minutes   Grilling: 30 minutes

1 chicken (1½ kg/3⅓ lb), cut
  into 6 pieces
1 heaped teaspoon turmeric powder
2 teaspoons salt

Ground Ingredients
20 dried chillies, soaked
12 shallots
5 cloves garlic
1¼ cm (½ in) ginger
2½ cm (1 in) young galingale
2½ cm (1 in) turmeric root

1 coconut, grated (for 1½ cups thick
  coconut milk)
1 teaspoon sugar
1 teaspoon salt
oil for deep-frying
1 stalk lemon grass, crushed lightly
  for basting

Rub chicken pieces with turmeric powder and salt and leave for 15 minutes. Combine ground ingredients, coconut milk, sugar and salt and keep aside.

Heat oil and deep-fry marinated chicken for 10 minutes or until half-cooked. Remove and drain well.

Using the crushed lemon grass, baste chicken with coconut mixture and grill, preferably over glowing charcoal. Baste chicken with coconut mixture at least 3 times on each side and grill until chicken is cooked.

Ayam Rendang Pedas

Preparation: 20 minutes   Cooking: 1 hour

1 chicken (2 kg/4½ lb), cut into bite-size
  pieces

Ground Ingredients
40 dried chillies, soaked
300 g (10 oz) shallots
4 cloves garlic
5 cm (2 in) ginger
6 stalks lemon grass
2½ cm (1 in) galingale
1 teaspoon turmeric powder

2 coconuts (for 4 cups thick coconut milk)
½ white coconut, grated for 'kerisik'
3 turmeric leaves ⎤
3 double lime leaves ⎟ *sliced finely*
2 teaspoons salt

Put chicken with ground ingredients in a *kuali*. Stir in coconut milk and bring to a slow boil.

Lower heat and simmer, stirring occasionally until gravy is thick. Add *kerisik* and stir continuously until meat is tender and gravy becomes very thick and oily. Lastly add sliced turmeric leaves and double lime leaves and salt to taste. Remove from heat.

Opposite: Ayam Panggang

Kurma Ayam

Preparation: 20 minutes   Cooking: 50 minutes

**1½ kg (3⅓ lb) chicken, cut into
    bite-size pieces**
1 teaspoon salt
6 tablespoons oil
5 shallots ⎤
1 clove garlic ⎦ *sliced*
2½ cm (1 in) ginger, cut into strips
**3 heaped tablespoons kurma curry powder,
    mixed to a paste with water**

Ground Ingredients
10 shallots
3 cloves garlic
2½ cm (1 in) ginger
4 tablespoons poppy seeds
1 tablespoon fennel
1 teaspoon cummin
1 tablespoon white peppercorns
2 tablespoons white grated coconut

Spices
2 sections of a star anise
5 cloves
2 cardamoms
2½ cm (1 in) stick cinnamon
¼ piece nutmeg

**1 coconut, grated (for 4 cups
    coconut milk)**
**3 onions, each slit across the top
    to form a flower (see diagram)**
3 sprigs Chinese celery, chopped
2 red chillies, sliced
2 tablespoons shallot crisps
1½ teaspoons salt

Season chicken with salt and leave aside.

Heat oil in an earthen pot and fry sliced shallots, garlic and ginger until fragrant. Add kurma curry paste and fry for a minute, then add ground ingredients and spices and continue frying until fragrant and oil appears on surface.

Put in chicken and fry for 5 minutes. Add coconut milk and onions. Bring to a boil, stirring constantly. Lower heat and simmer until chicken is tender. Just before removing from heat, add chopped celery, sliced chillies and shallot crisps. Stir in salt to taste.

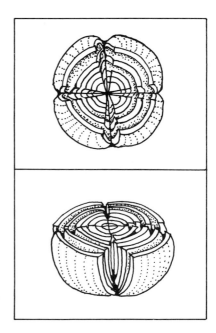

Rendang Ayam Perak

Preparation: 20 minutes   Cooking: 40 minutes

1 chicken (1½ kg/3⅓ lb), cut into bite-
   size pieces
2 teaspoons salt
5 tablespoons oil
2½ cm (1 in) galingale, crushed
3 stalks lemon grass, crushed

Ground Ingredients
20 dried chillies, soaked ⎫
3 red chillies, seeded ⎬ *ground together*
2½ cm (1 in) galingale
2½ cm (1 in) ginger
20 shallots
1 small pod garlic
2½ cm (1 in) turmeric root
3 stalks lemon grass

1½ coconuts (for 3 cups coconut milk)
2 turmeric leaves, sliced finely
1 teaspoon salt

Season chicken with salt and leave aside for 15 minutes.

Heat oil in a *kuali* and fry crushed galingale and lemon grass until fragrant. Fry ground chillies for 3-5 minutes, then other ground ingredients until fragrant and oil separates. Stir constantly to prevent mixture sticking to pan.

Pour in coconut milk and cook over low heat, stirring constantly for 10 minutes. When gravy is thickened, add chicken. Allow to simmer, stirring frequently until chicken is almost cooked. To prevent chicken from being overcooked, dish out chicken, leaving gravy to simmer till really thick. Put in chicken again and lastly turmeric leaves and salt. Remove from heat and serve with rice.

Note: This dish has very little gravy. Chicken must not be overcooked or Rendang will look messy with the flesh separated from the bones.

Kerabu Taugeh

Preparation: 20 minutes   Cooking: 10 minutes

600 g (1⅓ lb) beansprouts, tailed
1 tablespoon dried prawns, roasted and
   ground coarsely
2 tablespoons white grated coconut
   for 'kerisik'
6 shallots, sliced
20 bird chillies, sliced
juice of 1 large lime
½ coconut, grated (for 'pati santan')
½ teaspoon salt
¼ teaspoon monosodium glutamate

Scald beansprouts in boiling water and drain well. Combine beansprouts with remaining ingredients and mix well. Serve with boiled white rice.

Pecal (Vegetable Salad)

(photograph opposite)

Preparation: 30 minutes   Cooking: 20 minutes

300 g (10 oz) water convolvulus (young shoots only), cut into 5 cm (2 in) lengths
300 g (10 oz) young tapioca leaves (tender shoots only), cut into 5 cm (2 in) lengths
150 g (5 oz) beansprouts, tailed
150 g (5 oz) turnip, shredded coarsely
150 g (5 oz) long beans, cut into 5 cm (2 in) lengths
1 medium carrot, shredded coarsely
1 cucumber, soft centre discarded, shredded coarsely
2 firm soybean cakes, diced and fried
4 hardboiled eggs, quartered
1 tablespoon oil
2 tablespoons tamarind paste
½ cup water
1 tablespoon oil
15 dried chillies, soaked } *ground*
2½ cm (1 in) square dried shrimp paste, toasted } *ground*
1¼ cups water
4 tablespoons brown sugar
2 tablespoons black shrimp paste } *mixed*
1 tablespoon water } *mixed*
½ teaspoon salt
300 g (10 oz) roasted peanuts, ground coarsely
10 shallots } *sliced and fried*
3 cloves garlic } *sliced and fried*

Scald vegetables, except cucumber, separately in boiling water. Do not overcook. Drain well and arrange on a dish together with cucumber, fried soybean cakes and hardboiled eggs.

Heat 1 tablespoon oil and fry tamarind paste for 1 minute over low heat. Dish out, add water and mix well. Strain tamarind juice.

Heat 1 tablespoon oil and fry ground chillies and dried shrimp paste over low heat until fragrant. Add strained tamarind juice and water and bring to a boil. Stir in brown sugar, black shrimp paste and salt to taste. Remove from heat and stir in ground peanuts.

Garnish vegetables with shallot and garlic crisps. Serve with sauce or pour sauce over vegetables and mix well just before serving.

Kerabu Nenas

Preparation: 15 minutes   Cooking: 5 minutes

1 small pineapple, shredded coarsely
1 tablespoon dried prawns, roasted if desired } *ground*
4 red chillies } *ground*
½ coconut, grated (for 'pati santan')
½ teaspoon salt

Combine shredded pineapple with remaining ingredients and mix well. Serve with boiled white rice.

Opposite: Pecal

Ipoh Beansprouts with Saltfish

Preparation: 10 minutes   Cooking: 5 minutes

3 tablespoons oil
45 g (1½ oz) saltfish, preferably
   threadfin, washed and sliced finely
4 tablespoons oil
3 cloves garlic, minced
½ tablespoon light soy sauce
½ tablespoon sesame oil
300 g (10 oz) Ipoh beansprouts,
   washed and drained

Garnishing Ingredients
1 red chilli, seeded and cut
   into strips
1 stalk spring onion, split and cut into
   5 cm (2 in) lengths
1 sprig coriander leaves

Heat oil in a *kuali* until hot. Put in saltfish and fry over low heat until crisp and light golden brown. Drain and leave aside. Discard oil.

Heat 4 tablespoons oil in the same *kuali* and lightly brown garlic. Remove and place on a serving dish. Mix with light soy sauce and sesame oil.

Bring half a saucepan of water to a rapid boil. Put in beansprouts and scald for a few seconds. Drain well and place in the dish of prepared sauce. Mix to combine ingredients, then sprinkle with fried saltfish. Garnish with garnishing ingredients and serve hot.

Note: Ipoh beansprouts are especially crisp, fat and almost tailless. This has been attributed to the hardness of the underground water in the Ipoh district.

Pajri Nenas

Preparation: 15 minutes   Cooking: 15 minutes

1 medium pineapple
4 tablespoons oil
6 shallots   ⎫ sliced
2 cloves garlic   ⎭
1¼ cm (½ in) ginger, shredded
2½ cm (1 in) stick cinnamon
6 cloves
2 cardamoms
1 section of a star anise
3 tablespoons meat curry powder ⎫ mixed into
4 tablespoons water   ⎭ a paste
2 heaped tablespoons dried prawns,
   ground
5 tablespoons white grated coconut for
   'kerisik', ground
½ coconut, grated (for 2 cups
   coconut milk)
1 dessertspoon tamarind paste ⎫ mixed and
2 tablespoons water   ⎭ strained

1 teaspoon salt
1 teaspoon sugar
½ teaspoon monosodium glutamate

Halve the pineapple and cut into slices.

Heat oil in a *kuali* and lightly brown shallots, garlic and ginger, then add spices and fry until fragrant. Add curry powder paste, fry for 1 minute then add dried prawns and *kerisik*. Fry until fragrant. Put in pineapple slices, then pour in coconut milk and bring to a slow boil. Add tamarind juice, salt, sugar and monosodium glutamate. Simmer for 5 minutes and remove from heat.

Ipoh Sar Ho Fun (Rice Noodle Soup)

Preparation: 20 minutes Cooking: 40 minutes Serves: 5-6

450 g (1 lb) chicken, preferably thigh
   portion
1 teaspoon salt
½ teaspoon sesame oil
¼ teaspoon pepper
1 dessertspoon oil
2 tablespoons oil
4 cloves garlic, minced
600 g (1⅓ lb) large freshwater prawns,
   shells left on
8 cups anchovy or fresh chicken stock
3 teaspoons salt
1 teaspoon monosodium glutamate
1 tablespoon oil
90 g (3 oz) Chinese chives
600 g (1⅓ lb) flat rice noodles,
   cut into 6 mm (¼ in) strips
2 stalks spring onion, chopped
pepper

Season chicken with salt, sesame oil, pepper and 1 dessertspoon oil and leave for 15 minutes. Steam for 15 minutes until cooked. When cool, cut into 1¼ cm (½ in) thick slices and place on a serving dish.

Heat 2 tablespoons oil in a *kuali* and lightly brown garlic. Add prawns and stir-fry over high heat for 3 minutes until just cooked. Pour boiling anchovy or chicken stock into *kuali* and bring to a boil. Dish out prawns, shell and halve lengthwise. Place prawns on a serving dish.

Throw prawn shells into boiling stock and simmer over very low heat for 10 minutes to extract prawn flavour. Strain and put to boil again. Add salt and monosodium glutamate.

Boil half a saucepan of water with 1 tablespoon oil. Scald Chinese chives. Remove and cut into 5 cm (2 in) lengths. Place on serving dish. Boil rice noodles for 1-2 minutes. Drain well.

To serve, put small portions of rice noodles into individual bowls. Garnish with chicken and prawns. Pour boiling stock over noodles and serve hot sprinkled with spring onion, some chives and a dash of pepper.

Nasi Himpit

(photograph on page 98)

Preparation: 10 minutes Cooking: 20 minutes

2½ cups rice
5½ cups water
¼ teaspoon salt
3 screwpine leaves, knotted

Wash rice, drain and add water. Stir in salt and put in screwpine leaves. Cook rice till done. Stir and mash with a wooden spoon while still hot and moist.

Transfer rice to a 25 x 15 cm (10 x 6 in) rectangular dish or tin fitted with a flat lid a little smaller than dish or tin. Press lid firmly onto rice and place a heavy object on top to compress rice.

Leave for 6 hours or overnight in the refrigerator. Cut into 2½ cm (1 in) cubes and serve with Rendang Tok or any other Rendangs or Satay.

Fried Sar Ho Fun with Cockles

Preparation: 20 minutes   Cooking: 7 minutes   Serves: 3

300 g (10 oz) cockles
150 g (5 oz) prawns, shelled
½ teaspoon salt
¼ teaspoon pepper
3 tablespoons oil
3 cloves garlic
600 g (1⅓ lb) flat rice noodles,
    cut into 6 mm (¼ in) strips
150 g (5 oz) beansprouts, tailed
1 tablespoon dark soy sauce
2 tablespoons light soy sauce   } combined
½ teaspoon monosodium glutamate
1 tablespoon oil
2 eggs
4 tablespoons water
pepper

Pour boiling hot water over cockles and drain immediately. Remove flesh from shells. Season prawns with salt and pepper and leave aside.

Heat oil in a *kuali* until smoking hot, put in garlic and prawns and stir-fry quickly over high heat. Throw in noodles and stir-fry for 1-2 minutes, then add beansprouts. Stir to mix, add combined seasoning and fry for 1 minute. Push noodles to one side of *kuali,* add 1 tablespoon oil and break in eggs. Leave them for 30 seconds to set then stir-fry together with noodles and beansprouts.

Sprinkle water over noodles and stir-fry at the same time. Lastly, add cockles and fry for half a minute. Serve hot, sprinkled with a dash of pepper.

Puteri Berendam

Preparation: 15 minutes   Cooking: 20 minutes

Filling
60 g (2 oz) palm sugar, chopped
¼ cup water
pinch of salt
120 g (4 oz) white grated coconut

Dough
150 g (5 oz) glutinous rice flour
1 cup water
a few drops green colouring

Coconut Milk
1 coconut, grated (for 1½ cups thick
    coconut milk)
3 tablespoons sugar
¼ teaspoon salt
½ tablespoon flour
3 screwpine leaves, knotted

Put palm sugar, water and salt into a small saucepan over low heat and stir until palm sugar dissolves. Strain into a *kuali*, add grated coconut and fry till evenly coated with palm syrup. Dish out and cool.

Dough
Sift glutinous rice flour into a bowl, add water and knead into a firm dough together with green colouring. Form into small marble-size balls. Flatten each ball lightly and fill with a teaspoonful of filling. Press edges together and shape into small balls.

Boil half a saucepan of water and put in glutinous rice balls, a few at a time. As soon as they float to the surface, remove with a perforated ladle.

Coconut Milk
Mix coconut milk, sugar, salt and flour in a saucepan until smooth. Put in screwpine leaves and bring to a boil, stirring continuously. Put in glutinous rice balls and simmer for a few minutes until coconut milk thickens. Serve hot in small dishes.

Kuih Cara Berlauk (with Prawns)

Preparation: 20 minutes   Cooking: 1 hour   Makes: 60 small Kuih Cara

300 g (10 oz) small prawns,
    shelled and cut into small pieces
½ teaspoon salt
½ teaspoon monosodium glutamate
¼ teaspoon pepper
2 tablespoons oil
5 shallots, sliced finely
2 red chillies, seeded and
    sliced finely
1 stalk spring onion, chopped

Batter
300 g (10 oz) flour
1 coconut, grated (for 1³/₄ cups thick
    coconut milk)
2 eggs
1 teaspoon salt

Garnishing Ingredients
3 red chillies, seeded and sliced finely
1 stalk spring onion, chopped
reserved shallot crisps

Season prawns with salt, monosodium glutamate and pepper and leave for 15 minutes.

Heat oil in a *kuali* and lightly brown shallots. Drain and leave aside for garnishing.

Put seasoned prawns in the *kuali* and stir-fry for 2 minutes until cooked. Add red chillies and spring onion. Remove and cool.

Batter
Sift flour into a small mixing bowl. Stir in coconut milk a little at a time. Lightly beat eggs with a fork and mix into batter together with salt. Stir in cooled prawn mixture.

Grease and heat egg-shaped Kuih Cara mould over very low heat. Spoon 1 tablespoon prawn batter or enough to fill each individual mould and cook for 8-10 minutes.

When Kuih Cara is almost cooked, garnish with red chillies, spring onion and shallot crisps. Remove with a small butter knife when completely cooked.

Kuih Cara Berlauk (with Meat)

Preparation: 30 minutes   Cooking: 1 hour   Makes: 40-45 Kuih Cara

Filling
300 g (10 oz) beef, minced
3 tablespoons meat curry powder
2 tablespoons oil
2 onions, chopped finely
1 teaspoon salt
½ teaspoon monosodium glutamate

Batter
300 g (10 oz) flour
1 coconut, grated (for 1³/₄ cups thick coconut milk)
2 eggs
1 teaspoon salt

Garnishing Ingredients
3 red chillies, seeded and sliced finely
1 stalk spring onion, chopped finely

Season meat with curry powder.

Heat oil in a *kuali* and lightly brown onions. Add meat, salt and monosodium glutamate. Stir-fry till meat is cooked and dry. To prevent meat from sticking to pan, sprinkle a little water whilst frying. Remove and leave aside.

Batter
Sift flour into a small mixing bowl. Stir in coconut milk a little at a time until smooth. Lightly beat eggs with a fork and mix into batter together with salt.

Grease and heat a large egg-shaped Kuih Cara mould over low heat. Spoon ½ tablespoonful of batter into each individual mould then put in a teaspoonful of filling. Top with another tablespoonful of batter to cover filling and cook for approximately 10 minutes.

When Kuih Cara is almost cooked, garnish with red chillies and spring onion. Remove with a small knife when completely cooked.

Note: Kuih Cara moulds come in various sizes. For this recipe you will need a bigger egg-shaped mould to sandwich the filling.

Kuih Cara Manis

Preparation: 15 minutes   Cooking: 1 hour   Makes: 60 small Kuih Cara

300 g (10 oz) flour
1 coconut, grated (for 1³/₄ cups
   thick coconut milk)
1 tablespoon screwpine juice
2-3 drops green colouring
¼ teaspoon salt
2 eggs
castor sugar

Sift flour into a small mixing bowl. Stir in coconut milk a little at a time, together with screwpine juice, colouring and salt. Lightly beat eggs with a fork and stir into flour mixture.

Grease egg-shaped Kuih Cara mould with a little butter and heat over very low heat. Instead of spooning batter into each individual mould, which is time-consuming, pour batter into a measuring jug with a beak. This way, batter can be poured easily and quickly into moulds without spillage.

Fill each individual mould with batter and cook for approximately 8 minutes. When Kuih Cara is more than half-cooked, sprinkle a teaspoon of sugar evenly over surface of each. Remove with a small butter knife when completely cooked.

Note: To obtain screwpine juice easily, wash and cut 4-5 leaves into small pieces and blend with a little water. Strain to get clear juice.

KELANTAN

Kelantan ('land of lightning') is situated in the northeast of Peninsular Malaysia. The coastal beaches which extend for miles are famous for their shimmering white sand dotted here and there by serene fishing *kampungs* whose occupants are noted for their strong and varied cultural activities. The people here are predominantly Malay and their economic life centres around offshore fishing and padi growing further inland on low fertile plains.

Isolated from the west of the Peninsula by the main mountain range and by strong monsoon winds from the South China Sea which bring heavy rainfall at the end and beginning of the year, Kelantan has bred a tough weathered people steeped in cultural heritage. Prominent cultural activities like the *makyung* and *menora* dance drama are exclusive to Kelantan. Of particular note too are the *wayang kulit* or shadow play and *bersilat,* the Malay art of self-defence.

The most famous handicrafts which form the basis of many cottage industries are the exquisite silverware, *kain songket,* with intricately hand-woven gold and silver threads, and handprinted *batik* in beautiful chromatic designs. Top spinning (*main gasing*) and kite (*wau*) flying are two favourite pastimes which have been elevated by skilled craftsmanship. Both are gay and spellbinding spectacles.

As exotic as their handicrafts is Kelantanese food, aromatic, enlivened with chillies and lots of shallots, mildly spiced and slightly sweet. Their Nasi Dagang — a unique rice with a brownish tinge steamed with coconut milk, Ayam Percik and Kuzi Ayam are East Coast specials. Kelantanese cooking may be slightly sweet but sugar can always be omitted from some dishes if natural sweetness from meat and coconut is preferred.

Opposite: Kerabu Sotong Kering

Solok Lada

Preparation: 20 minutes   Cooking: 15 minutes

16 large red chillies
180 g (6 oz) spanish mackerel,
    meat only
150 g (5 oz) white grated coconut
shallots
1 teaspoon sugar
1 teaspoon salt
³/₄ coconut, grated (for ³/₄ cup coconut milk)
pinch of salt

Slit chillies lengthwise with a sharp knife for stuffing. Carefully remove seeds and soak in water for 15 minutes.

Cut fish meat into large cubes and place in an electric chopper with grated coconut and shallots. Blend until fine. Stir in sugar and salt and mix well.

Stuff each chilli with 1 tablespoonful of fish mixture. Place chillies, slit side up, in a pot. Carefully pour in coconut milk mixed with salt. Cover pot and simmer gently for 15 minutes until cooked and almost dry.

Note: Serve Solok Lada with rice or Nasi Kerabu (page 129).

Kerabu Sotong Kering

(photograph on page 116)

Preparation: 20 minutes   Cooking: 1 minute

90 g (3 oz) dried cuttlefish flakes
1 small green mango, skinned and cut into
    strips
½ cucumber, seed portion removed,
    shredded
2 red chillies, sliced finely
6 bird chillies, sliced finely
7 shallots, sliced finely
juice of 3-4 large limes
2 tablespoons sugar or to taste
oil for deep-frying

Wash cuttlefish, drain and dry in the sun or in a slow oven. Combine remaining ingredients (except oil) in a bowl then leave to drain in a colander for 1 hour.

Heat oil in a *kuali* and deep-fry flaked cuttlefish until light golden and crisp. Drain and cool.

Just before serving, combine cuttlefish crisps with other ingredients. Serve on a flat dish.

Note: Prepared flaked cuttlefish is sold in packets and easily obtainable in Kelantan and Trengganu.

Daging Goreng Pengantin

Preparation: 1 hour   Cooking: 1¼ hours

1 kg (2¹/₅ lb) beef
2 teaspoons salt
2 pieces dried tamarind skin
6 tablespoons oil
300 g (10 oz) shallots, sliced
30 dried chillies, ground coarsely
1¼ x 2½ cm (½ x 1 in) ginger ⎫ *ground*
1 tablespoon coriander ⎭ *finely*
1½ coconuts (for 1⅓ cups 'pati santan')
1½ teaspoons sugar
1½ teaspoons salt
½ teaspoon monosodium glutamate

Note: Daging Goreng Pengantin can be stored for a couple of weeks to accompany and make a rice meal more appetising. Served on buttered toast and in sandwiches, they make tasty though quite 'unKelantanese' snacks.

Cut beef into 5 x 2½ cm (2 x 1 in) pieces. Put beef, salt and dried tamarind skin in a large pot with enough water to cover meat. Cover and simmer for 1 hour or pressure cook for 35 minutes. Remove and drain in a colander until dry and cool. Lightly pound meat with a pestle, then using fingers break meat into small pieces.

Heat oil in a *kuali* and brown shallots. Remove shallot crisps with a perforated ladle and drain.

Remove oil, leaving 2 tablespoons in the *kuali*. Fry ground chillies, ginger and coriander over low heat until oil separates. Add *pati santan*, sugar, salt and monosodium glutamate. Bring to a slow boil and simmer until thick. Put in meat and fry continuously for 40 minutes until almost dry. Put in shallot crisps and fry over very low heat for 15 minutes until dry and meat is almost crisp.

Remove and cool on absorbent paper. When thoroughly cooled, store in an airtight container.

Daging Masak Lawar

Preparation: 25 minutes   Cooking: 15 minutes

600 g (1⅓ lb) beef fillet
4-5 tablespoons white grated coconut for 'kerisik', ground

Ground Ingredients
1 tablespoon coriander, roasted
8 red chillies
16 shallots
2½ cm (1 in) ginger

juice of 3 large limes
1 coconut, grated (for 1 cup 'pati santan')
1½ teaspoons salt
1 teaspoon monosodium glutamate

Boil half a saucepan of water, put in beef and boil until cooked. Drain and when cooled, slice into thin 4 cm (1½ in) strips.

In a cooking pot mix ground *kerisik*, ground ingredients, lime juice, *pati santan* and sliced beef together. Bring to a slow boil. Lower heat and simmer, stirring frequently, until gravy is thick. Add salt and monosodium glutamate.

Rendang Daging

Preparation: 20 minutes   Cooking: 1 hour

**1½ kg (3⅓ lb) beef, scored and cut into
2½ x 5 cm (1 x 2 in) cubes**

Ground Ingredients
15 red bird chillies
15 green bird chillies
300 g (10 oz) shallots
10 cloves garlic
2½ x 5 cm (1 x 2 in) ginger
2½ x 4 cm (1 x 1½ in) galingale
2½ x 5 cm (1 x 2 in) turmeric root
5 stalks lemon grass

**3 coconuts, grated (for 3 cups 'pati santan'
and 3 cups thin coconut milk)**
4 double lime leaves ⎤
⎟ *sliced finely*
4 turmeric leaves ⎦
3 pieces dried tamarind skin
2 teaspoons salt
**1 teaspoon sugar or monosodium
glutamate**

Marinate meat with ground ingredients and leave for 15 minutes. Put marinated beef and thin coconut milk in a pressure cooker and cook for 30 minutes.

At the end of that time, add thick coconut milk and bring to a boil. Lower heat and simmer till gravy is almost thick. Add double lime and turmeric leaves and dried tamarind skin and simmer, stirring continuously, until meat is tender and gravy thick. Add salt and monosodium glutamate to taste.

Daging Masak Merah

Preparation: 30 minutes   Cooking: 1¼ hours

**600 g (1⅓ lb) beef, scored and cut into
4 cm (1½ in) cubes**
5 cm (2 in) ginger ⎤
⎟ *ground*
5 cm (2 in) turmeric root ⎦
8 tablespoons oil
450 g (1 lb) shallots, sliced and fried crisp
120 g (4 oz) cashew nuts
90 g (3 oz) sultanas
40 dried chillies, soaked and ground
5 cups water
2-3 jackfruit leaves
1 large can (410 g/15 oz) evaporated milk
½ can (140 g/5 oz) tomato puree
4 tablespoons tomato sauce
**2 teaspoons tamarind paste, mixed with a
little water and strained**
2 teaspoons salt
a few sprigs mint leaves
2 sprigs coriander leaves ⎤ *cut into 2½ cm*
2 stalks spring onion ⎦ *(1 in) lengths*
1 teaspoon sugar or monosodium glutamate

Marinate beef with ground ginger and turmeric and leave aside.

Heat oil. Lightly brown shallots until crisp. Remove with a perforated ladle and keep aside. Reheat oil and fry cashew nuts until lightly browned. Drain. Put in sultanas and fry for 1 minute. Remove and drain. Put in ground chillies and fry till oil separates. Dish out and leave aside.

Put in beef, add water and jackfruit leaves and bring to a boil. Lower heat and simmer for 1 hour till beef is tender. Discard jackfruit leaves. Put in crispy shallots, cashew nuts, sultanas, ground chillies and all remaining ingredients. Simmer, stirring frequently, till gravy is thick and meat tender.

Note: Jackfruit leaves are used as tenderizer.

Roast Tongue

Preparation: 30 minutes   Cooking: 1¼ hours   Oven setting: 175°C, 350°F, Gas Regulo 6

1 cow's tongue
2½ x 5 cm (1 x 2 in) turmeric root, ground
2 teaspoons salt
1 dessertspoon vinegar
2 dessertspoons light soy sauce
1 dessertspoon pepper
½ teaspoon salt
1 teaspoon monosodium glutamate
3 tablespoons tapioca flour mixed with a
    little water
3 potatoes, halved

Scald tongue in boiling water. Drain and scrape off skin with a knife. Prick tongue with a skewer, then rub with ground turmeric and salt and leave for 15 minutes.

Place tongue in a pressure cooker with enough water to cover and pressure cook for 45 minutes. Drain and season with vinegar, soy sauce, pepper, salt, monosodium glutamate and tapioca flour paste.

Put tongue with seasoning sauce and potatoes in a baking dish and roast in a moderate oven for 30 minutes until tongue is tender and potatoes cooked.

Remove tongue and cut into thin slices. Arrange on a dish, with potatoes. Pour pan sauce over sliced tongue and garnish with spring onion and chillies.

Kerabu Perut

Preparation: 20 minutes   Cooking: 1 hour

1 kg (2¹/₅ lb) tripe
salt
5 tablespoons white grated coconut for
    'kerisik', ground coarsely
10 shallots, sliced
5 red chillies, seeded and sliced
1 small bunch polygonum leaves, sliced
    finely
juice of 3 large limes
3 tablespoons white grated coconut
1½ teaspoons salt
1 teaspoon sugar or monosodium
    glutamate
½ coconut, grated (for ½ cup 'pati santan')

Clean and rub tripe with salt. Put in a saucepan of water and boil until tender. Drain and slice into 1¼ cm (½ in) strips.

Place tripe in a mixing bowl and mix with remaining ingredients. *Pati santan* should only be added just before serving.

Kuzi Ayam

(photograph opposite)

Preparation: 40 minutes   Cooking: 45 minutes

1½ kg (3⅓ lb) chicken, cut into 4-6 pieces
a few saffron strands ⎤
1 teaspoon water ⎬ ground
600 g (1⅓ lb) shallots, sliced and
    fried crisp

Ground Ingredients
1 tablespoon coriander
1 dessertspoon fennel
1 dessertspoon cummin
1 dessertspoon peppercorns
1 piece mace
5 cardamoms
5 cloves
2½ cm (1 in) ginger
2½ cm (1 in) stick cinnamon
2½ cm (1 in) turmeric root
3 slices galingale

1 large can (410 g/15 oz) ⎤
    evaporated milk ⎬ combined
juice of 3 small limes ⎦
4 cups water
8 tablespoons oil
60 g (2 oz) sultanas
2 dessertspoons ghee
5 shallots ⎤
3 cloves garlic ⎬ sliced
4 tablespoons tomato sauce

2 teaspoons salt
20 roasted almonds
1 teaspoon sugar or monosodium
    glutamate

Wash and dry chicken and rub with ground saffron. (If saffron is not available use a few drops of yellow colouring.)

In a large bowl, combine shallot crisps with ground ingredients, evaporated milk and lime mixture and water. Leave aside.

Heat oil in a *kuali* and fry sultanas for a minute. Remove and drain. Add half the ghee to *kuali* and fry chicken for 15 minutes. Dish out and drain.

Pour oil into a curry pot, add remaining ghee and brown sliced shallots and garlic. Add ground ingredients and evaporated milk mixture, tomato sauce and salt. Bring to a boil, stirring frequently, then add half the fried sultanas, half the almonds, and sugar or monosodium glutamate. Simmer until mixture thickens, then add fried chicken and cook over moderate heat until gravy is thick and oil appears on surface. Serve sprinkled with remaining sultanas and almonds.

Ros Ayam

Preparation: 15 minutes   Cooking: 40 minutes

oil for deep-frying
1 chicken (1½ kg/3⅓ lb), cut into
    4-6 pieces
4 cups water
15 shallots, sliced and fried crisp
5 cloves garlic, sliced and fried crisp
1 small can (170 g/6 oz) evaporated milk
4 potatoes, halved
3 onions, cut into wedges
10 stalks Chinese chives, cut into
    4 cm (1½ in) lengths
4 red chillies, sliced
2 teaspoons salt

Heat oil in a *kuali* and deep-fry chicken for 10 minutes until lightly browned. Boil water in a saucepan and put in fried chicken. Bring to a boil then simmer over low heat for 10 minutes.

Combine half the shallot and garlic crisps with evaporated milk and add to chicken. Bring to a boil then put in potatoes and onions.

When chicken is tender, add Chinese chives, red chillies and salt to taste. Dish out and serve hot, sprinkled with remaining shallot and garlic crisps.

Opposite: Kuzi Ayam and Nasi Dagang

Ayam Percik

Preparation: 15 minutes   Cooking: 10 minutes   Grilling: 15-20 minutes

1½ kg (3⅓ lb) chicken, cut into
    4 large pieces
2½ cm (1 in) ginger ⎱ ground
4 cloves garlic ⎰
1 teaspoon salt
1½ coconuts, grated (for 3 cups coconut
    milk)
1 heaped tablespoon rice flour
8 dried chillies, soaked ⎫
8 shallots ⎪
1¼ cm (½ in) ginger ⎬ ground
2½ cm (1 in) square ⎪
    dried shrimp paste ⎭
1 tablespoon tamarind paste ⎱ mixed and
4 tablespoons water ⎰ strained
1 teaspoon salt
1 teaspoon sugar

Marinate chicken with ground ginger and garlic and salt and leave for 1 hour.

Mix coconut milk with rice flour, ground ingredients and tamarind juice and bring to a slow boil. Add salt and sugar and keep stirring over low heat for 10 minutes until thickened.

Dip chicken in thick coconut gravy and place over glowing charcoal grill, basting chicken frequently with more coconut milk for approximately 15 minutes or until both sides are evenly browned and chicken is cooked.

Kelantanese Egg Curry

(photograph opposite)

Preparation: 15 minutes   Cooking: 30 minutes

8 tablespoons oil
5 shallots ⎱ sliced
5 cloves garlic ⎰

Ground Ingredients
20 dried chillies, soaked
4 cm (1½ in) ginger
4 cm (1½ in) galingale
4 cm (1½ in) turmeric root
4 stalks lemon grass
30 peppercorns
2 tablespoons coriander

2 coconuts, grated (for 4 cups
    coconut milk, or sufficient
    coconut milk to cover eggs)
4 pieces dried tamarind skin
20 hardboiled eggs
6 tomatoes, cut into wedges
6 red chillies ⎱ left whole
6 green chillies ⎰

2½ teaspoons salt
1 teaspoon sugar or monosodium
    glutamate

Heat oil in a *kuali* and brown shallots and garlic. Add ground ingredients and fry until fragrant and oil separates.

Pour in coconut milk, add dried tamarind skin and bring to a slow boil. Put in hardboiled eggs, tomatoes, red and green chillies. Add salt to taste and monosodium glutamate and when it boils again remove from heat.

Note: To shell eggs easily, add a little vinegar when boiling.

Opposite: Kelantanese Egg Curry

Ayam Masak Keremak

Preparation: 20 minutes   Cooking: 30 minutes

1½ kg (3⅓ lb) chicken, cut into
    bite-size pieces

Ground Ingredients
3 tablespoons coriander
3 tablespoons poppy seeds
2 teaspoons fennel
2 teaspoons cummin
2 teaspoons pepper
10 cashew nuts

1½ teaspoons salt
4 tablespoons oil
2 tablespoons ghee
20 shallots, sliced
5 cloves garlic
1¼ cm (½ in) stick cinnamon
5 cloves
5 cardamoms
3 pieces mace
1 coconut, grated (for 1 cup thick
    coconut milk and 3 cups thin
    coconut milk)
3 red chillies   } *left whole*
3 green chillies
3 tomatoes, halved
3 tablespoons evaporated milk
juice of 1 large lime
2 teaspoons salt

Marinate chicken with ground ingredients and salt and leave for 30 minutes.

Heat oil and ghee in a curry pot and lightly brown shallots and garlic, then add spices and fry until fragrant. Put in marinated meat and stir-fry till almost dry. Pour in thin coconut milk and bring to a boil. Lower heat and simmer for 15 minutes. Add chillies, tomatoes, thick coconut milk, evaporated milk and lime juice. Simmer for another 5 minutes. When meat is tender, add salt to taste.

Ayam Kerutuk

Preparation: 20 minutes   Cooking: 40 minutes

1½ kg (3⅓ lb) chicken
4 tablespoons oil
10 shallots, sliced
45 g (1½ oz) dried chillies, soaked
  and ground
4 tablespoons grated white coconut for
  'kerisik'

Ground Ingredients
2 tablespoons coriander powder
5 cardamoms
5 cloves
1 teaspoon fennel
1 teaspoon cummin
1 teaspoon black peppercorns
1¼ cm (½ in) stick cinnamon
4 cm (1½ in) turmeric root
4 cm (1½ in) galingale
5 x 2½ cm (2 x 1 in) ginger
2 stalks lemon grass
5 cloves garlic

2 pieces dried tamarind skin
1 coconut, grated (for 4 cups
  coconut milk)
1 teaspoon sugar or monosodium
  glutamate

Cut chicken into 4-8 large pieces.

Heat oil in a cooking pot and fry sliced shallots and half the ground chillies. Remove and leave aside.

Combine ground *kerisik* with remaining ground chillies and ground ingredients. Marinate chicken with this mixture and leave for 15 minutes.

Place marinated chicken in the cooking pot, add dried tamarind skin and bring to a slow boil over medium heat, stirring gently. When liquid is semi-dry pour in coconut milk. Bring to a boil then simmer over low heat, stirring constantly for 15 minutes or until gravy is half-dry. Add fried shallots and chillies and seasoning. Allow to simmer for 20 minutes until chicken is tender and oil appears on surface.

Solo Itik

Preparation: 30 minutes   Cooking: 1¼ hours

1 duck (1½ kg/3⅓ lb)
15 x 2½ cm (6 x 1 in) turmeric
    root, ground
2 teaspoons salt
6 stalks lemon grass   ⎫ *crushed*
15 x 2½ cm (6 x 1 in) ginger   ⎬ *lightly*
10 cm (4 in) stick cinnamon
7 cloves
8 cardamoms

Ground Ingredients

1 tablespoon coriander
1 teaspoon fennel
1 teaspoon cummin
3 cloves
2 cardamoms
2 pieces mace
10 black peppercorns
20 dried chillies, soaked
30 shallots
5 cm (2 in) galingale
2½ cm (1 in) ginger

2 tablespoons white grated coconut
    for 'kerisik', ground coarsely
2 coconuts, grated (for 2½ cups thick
    coconut milk)
2 tablespoons rice flour, mixed till
    smooth with ½ cup water or thin
    coconut milk
1 teaspoon salt
10 shallots, sliced and fried crisp,
    crushed lightly
1 sugarcane, approx. 90 cm
    (3 feet) long
lettuce
cucumber
chillies

Wash and clean duck thoroughly. Season with ground turmeric and salt for 15 minutes, then rinse under a running tap. Stitch the openings of duck, leaving 2½ cm (1 in) at the neck and the end for sugarcane pole to go through.

In a large pot, put in duck, crushed lemon grass, ginger, cinnamon, cloves and cardamoms. Add enough water to cover duck and bring to a slow boil. Lower heat and simmer duck for ¾ hour or until duck is just tender. Remove and drain.

Reserve two tablespoons of ground ingredients. In a saucepan, mix remaining ground ingredients with *kerisik,* thick coconut milk, rice batter and salt. Bring this mixture to a slow boil. Lower heat and simmer, stirring continuously until gravy is thick. Stir in lightly crushed shallot crisps. If short of time, this basting gravy can be prepared a day ahead and refrigerated.

To barbecue duck, cut 3 diagonal slits across back and breast of duck with a sharp knife. Rub reserved ground ingredients over duck and leave for 15 minutes. Allow duck to cool thoroughly.

Thread duck through the sugarcane pole and spoon boiled gravy over duck. Barbecue over glowing charcoal pit, rotating the sugarcane pole to brown duck evenly. Repeat basting twice and cook till duck is done.

Remove from pole and serve hot, garnished with lettuce, cucumber and chillies.

Nasi Kerabu

Preparation: 40 minutes   Cooking: 45 minutes   Serves: 8

2-3 mackerels, grilled and flaked

Ground Ingredients
8 shallots
2½ cm (1 in) ginger
¼ teaspoon pepper

1 white coconut, grated for 'kerisik'
½ teaspoon salt
1 teaspoon sugar

Sauce
1 coconut, grated (for 4 cups coconut milk)
10 dried chillies, soaked ⎱ *ground*
8 shallots ⎰
2 pieces dried tamarind skin
2 stalks lemon grass, crushed lightly
1 teaspoon sugar
1 teaspoon salt

Garnishing Ingredients
1 cucumber, shredded
5-6 sprigs polygonum leaves, sliced finely
6 long beans, sliced finely
2 stalks lemon grass, sliced finely
10 young cashewnut leaves, sliced finely

Side Dish
8 small-medium mackerels
1 teaspoon salt
1 teaspoon tamarind paste ⎱ *mixed and*
2 tablespoons water ⎰ *strained*
1 cup rice flour
½ cup water ⎱ *blend till*
½ teaspoon turmeric powder ⎰ *smooth*
pinch of salt
oil

sufficient cooked rice for 8 persons

Put flaked fish, ground ingredients and *kerisik* into a mixing bowl. Add salt and sugar and mix well. Place in a serving dish.

Sauce
Put coconut milk, ground ingredients, tamarind skin and lemon grass in a pot and bring to a slow boil. Simmer gently, stirring constantly for 10 minutes until oil appears on the surface. Add sugar and salt and put in a serving bowl.

Garnishing Ingredients
Arrange garnishing ingredients attractively on a dish.

Side Dish
Rub fish with salt and tamarind juice and leave for 15 minutes. Dip fish into batter and fry in hot oil for 2-3 minutes on each side until cooked and light golden. Place on a serving dish.

Serving
To serve Nasi Kerabu, put enough rice on a plate and pile on as much flaked fish with coconut, sauce and as many garnishing ingredients as desired. Mix with rice and take with a fried fish.

Laksa Kelantan

(photograph opposite)

Preparation: 30 minutes   Cooking: 40 minutes   Serves: 10 approximately

1 kg (2¹/₅ lb) mackerel
2 teaspoons salt
1 coconut, grated (for 8½ cups coconut
   milk)

Ground Ingredients
15 dried chillies, soaked
2½ cm (1 in) galingale
1¼ cm (½ in) ginger
2½ cm (1 in) turmeric root
1 teaspoon black peppercorns

15 shallots ⎫ sliced
3 cloves garlic ⎭
10 stalks polygonum leaves
1 wild ginger flower, split
4 pieces dried tamarind skin
2 teaspoons salt
1 teaspoon sugar
1 teaspoon monosodium glutamate
1½ packets fresh thick rice vermicelli,
   scalded in boiling hot water and
   drained

Garnishing Ingredients
2 cucumbers, soft centres discarded,
   peeled and shredded
300 g (10 oz) beansprouts,
   tailed and scalded
8 long beans, cut into 2½ cm (1 in) lengths
   and scalded
5-6 stalks polygonum leaves, stalks
   discarded, washed
1 wild ginger flower, sliced
1 small bunch mint leaves
1 small bunch basil leaves

Season fish with salt and leave for 15 minutes. Steam, flake and blend fish coarsely with coconut milk, one third at a time.

Put blended fish and coconut milk in a pot with ground and sliced ingredients and bring to a boil. Lower heat and simmer for 10 minutes. Add polygonum leaves, wild ginger flower, dried tamarind skin, salt, sugar and monosodium glutamate and simmer for 20 minutes, stirring frequently.

To serve, put a little thick rice vermicelli into individual serving dishes, garnish with a little of each garnishing ingredient. Pour hot fish gravy over this. Serve hot.

Note: Do not throw away the wild ginger flower stems. Lightly smash the stems and simmer in gravy. Discard when gravy is ready to be served.

Opposite: Laksa Kelantan

Nasi Dagang

(photograph on page 122)

Preparation: 15 minutes   Cooking: 1 hour

4 cups Nasi Dagang rice ('beras lembut')
   or 3 cups (700 g/1½ lb) good grade
   Siamese rice with 1 cup (240 g/8 oz)
   glutinous rice
1½ coconuts, grated (for 1½ cups
   'pati santan' and 1½ cups thin
   coconut milk)
10 shallots, sliced
2½ cm (1 in) ginger, shredded
¼ teaspoon fenugreek
1 teaspoon salt

Wash rice and leave to soak overnight. The next day, drain and steam rice mixture for half an hour. Stir in thin coconut milk and resteam for 15 minutes until the rice is nearly cooked.

Combine *pati santan* with shallots, ginger, fenugreek and salt and stir into cooked rice. Resteam again for another 15 minutes or until rice is properly cooked.

Note: Beras lembut is a special rice for Nasi Dagang and it has a brownish tinge.

Taihi Itik

Preparation: 5 minutes   Cooking: 15 minutes

5 egg whites
180 g (6 oz) sugar
1½ teaspoons flour
2 screwpine leaves, knotted
4 cloves

Strain egg whites through a fine sieve into a mixing bowl. Stir in sugar and flour until sugar is dissolved.

Pour egg white mixture into a small saucepan. Add screwpine leaves and cloves and stir over low heat with a wooden spoon until dry and mixture is of custard consistency. Serve hot or cold spread on toast.

Jemput Durian

Preparation: 10 minutes Cooking: 5 minutes Makes: 20

1 egg
15 g (½ oz) sugar
¼ teaspoon salt
90 g (3 oz) self-raising flour ⎫ *sifted*
1 teaspoon baking powder   ⎬ *together*
30 g (1 oz) cornflour   ⎭
½ cup water or milk
180 g (6 oz) durian pulp from
    1 small durian
oil for deep-frying

Whisk egg and sugar until light and fluffy. Add salt and fold in sifted ingredients alternately with water or milk. Add durian pulp and mix well.

Heat oil in a *kuali* for deep-frying. Fry tablespoonfuls of batter over very low heat until dark golden brown. Drain well before serving.

TRENGGANU

Unspoilt beauty, refreshing and unhurried, gentle and tranquil with long stretches of sparkling white, palm-fringed beaches: these are some of the attributes of Trengganu.

The idyllic coastline abounds with quaint, peaceful fishing villages, the mastery of their craftsmen reflected in the intricate *bangaus* (mastheads) of skilfully carved boats.

Apart from access to the sea, a rich fishing ground for local fishermen, the beaches in this vicinity are reputed to be the most rewarding for turtle-watching when turtles make their trek up the beach to lay eggs, a ritual occurring every year around August.

As in Kelantan, the people of Trengganu are well-known for their handicrafts, like silk and songket weaving, brassware and *mengkuang* weaving which make up their main cottage industries.

In Trengganu, one should not fail to experience Malay cuisine which is unique to the East Coast.

Their Ayam Percik which is grilled is popular and the style of cooking shows a Thai influence. Nasi Ulam — rice mixed with a variety of tender shoots and vegetables, all finely cut and accompanied by a coconut sambal, their highly spiced Daging Kerutut Kering and Rendang are just samples of tempting dishes which are as reputable as their *wayang kulit* and sinuous *kris*.

Opposite: Daging Kerutut Kering

Sambal Ikan Kembung

(photograph opposite)

Preparation: 20 minutes   Cooking: 1 hour 5 minutes

1 kg (2¹/₅ lb) mackerel or horse mackerel
1½ coconuts, grated (for 1½ cups
  'pati santan')

Ground Ingredients
15 red chillies
4 cm (1½ in) ginger
15 shallots
2 cloves garlic

2 large pieces dried tamarind skin
1 teaspoon monosodium glutamate
2 teaspoons salt
2 teaspoons sugar

Steam fish for 12 minutes or until cooked. When cool, remove bones and lightly mash fish with the back of a spoon.

Combine *pati santan* with ground ingredients, tamarind skin, monosodium glutamate, salt, sugar and mashed fish. Bring to a slow boil over moderate heat for 5 minutes, stirring frequently.

Lower heat and fry continuously for approximately 50 minutes, taking care mixture does not stick to pan, until completely dry.

Note: Sambal Ikan Kembung is like meat floss and is quite crisp out of the pan.

Beef Rendang, Trengganu Style

Preparation: 20 minutes   Cooking: 1¼ hours

600 g (1⅓ lb) beef, cut into 6 mm x 5 cm
  (¼ x 2 in) slices

Ground Ingredients
25 dried chillies, soaked
16 shallots
2 cloves garlic
2 stalks lemon grass, sliced
1¼ cm (½ in) ginger
1¼ cm (½ in) galingale

2 coconuts, grated (for 5 cups coconut
  milk)
1 large turmeric leaf
1 double lime leaf, sliced
120 g (4 oz) white grated coconut for
  'kerisik'

Marinate beef with ground ingredients and leave for 15 minutes.

In a *kuali,* mix together coconut milk and marinated beef. Place over medium heat and bring to a slow boil, stirring occasionally.

Lower heat and simmer for 1 hour, stirring frequently, until gravy is thick.

Put in turmeric leaf, sliced lime leaf and *kerisik* and stir continuously for another 15 minutes until very little gravy remains.

Opposite: Sambal Ikan Kembung

Daging Kerutut Kering

(photograph on page 134)

Preparation: 25 minutes   Cooking: 50 minutes to 1 hour

1 kg (2¹/₅ lb) beef or 1½ kg (3⅓ lb) chicken
8 tablespoons oil
1 onion, sliced
1¼ cm (½ in) stick cinnamon
2 cardamoms
3 cloves

Ground Ingredients
20 dried chillies, soaked
12 shallots
4 cloves garlic
2½ cm (1 in) turmeric root
1¼ cm (½ in) ginger
2 heaped tablespoons coriander
2 teaspoons fennel
1 teaspoon cummin
1¼ cm (½ in) stick cinnamon
2 sections of a star anise
3 cardamoms
3 cloves
12 black peppercorns

1 coconut, grated (for 3 cups coconut
    milk)
2 pieces dried tamarind skin
1 heaped teaspoon sugar
3 screwpine leaves, knotted
4 tablespoons white grated coconut
    for 'kerisik'
2 teaspoons salt

Cut beef across the grain into thin slices 4 cm (1½ in) wide. If using chicken, cut into 8 pieces.

Heat oil in a *kuali* until hot and fry onion and spices until fragrant. Put in ground ingredients and fry over moderate heat until fragrant and oil separates.

Add beef or chicken and continue frying for 3 minutes, then pour in coconut milk. Add tamarind skin, sugar and screwpine leaves and simmer over low heat for 40 minutes, stirring frequently until meat is tender and gravy thick. Put in *kerisik* and salt and stir-fry until very little gravy remains.

Discard tamarind skin and screwpine leaves.

Ayam Terutuk

Preparation: 20 minutes   Cooking: 40 minutes

1½ kg (3⅓ lb) chicken
1 coconut, grated (for 3 cups coconut
  milk)

Ground Ingredients
35 dried chillies, soaked
3 cloves garlic
12 shallots
2½ cm (1 in) galingale
2½ cm (1 in) turmeric root
1¼ cm (½ in) ginger
2 tablespoons coriander
1 tablespoon fennel
4 cloves
4 cardamoms

4 tablespoons white grated coconut for
  'kerisik'
1 tablespoon tamarind paste ⎫ *mixed and*
¼ cup water   ⎭ *strained*
1 teaspoon sugar
2 teaspoons salt

Cut chicken into 8 pieces and drain in a colander.

Put coconut milk, ground ingredients and *kerisik* into a pot and bring to a boil. Stir in tamarind juice.

Put in chicken and cook over low heat, stirring frequently until chicken is tender and gravy thickens. Add sugar and salt to taste.

Ayam Golek

Preparation: 15 minutes   Cooking: 30 minutes   Baking: 30 minutes   Oven setting: 175°C, 350°F, Gas Regulo 6

1 chicken (1½ kg/3⅓ lb)
2 teaspoons salt

Ground Ingredients
12 shallots
3 cloves garlic
3 stalks lemon grass
5 cm (2 in) galingale
2½ cm (1 in) ginger
1 teaspoon white peppercorns
1 teaspoon cummin
1 tablespoon fennel

1 coconut, grated (for 3 cups coconut
  milk)
1 teaspoon salt
½ teaspoon monosodium glutamate

Rub chicken with salt and leave aside.

Mix ground ingredients with coconut milk in a *kuali*. Bring to a slow boil then put in chicken and seasoning. Simmer over low heat for 30 minutes, turning chicken halfway through cooking.

When gravy thickens transfer chicken and gravy into a heatproof oven dish and bake in a moderate oven for 30 minutes until chicken is cooked through and lightly browned.

Serve hot, garnished with red chillies if desired.

Ayam Percik

Preparation: 30 minutes   Cooking: 15 minutes   Grilling: 30 minutes

1 chicken (1½ kg/3⅓ lb), cut into
   6-8 pieces
1 heaped teaspoon black peppercorns, ground
1 heaped teaspoon salt
½ teaspoon monosodium glutamate
4 tablespoons oil

Ground Ingredients
20 shallots
5 candlenuts
1 tablespoon coriander
½ dessertspoon fennel
½ dessertspoon cummin
3 stalks lemon grass
5 cm (2 in) galingale

2 coconuts, grated (for 2½ cups 'pati
   santan')
½ teaspoon salt
1 teaspoon light soy sauce

Season chicken with black pepper, salt and monosodium glutamate for at least an hour.

Heat oil in a *kuali* and fry ground ingredients until fragrant. Put in *pati santan,* salt and light soy sauce and simmer over low heat for 8-10 minutes until thick and oil appears on surface. Drain chicken. Coat with this thick gravy and place on charcoal grill, basting chicken frequently with more gravy until cooked.

Serve with boiled white rice or Nasi Minyak and a cucumber salad.

Note: Ayam Percik tastes very much like Chicken Satay.

Kurma Ayam

Preparation: 30 minutes   Cooking: 30 minutes

1½ kg (3⅓ lb) chicken, cut into bite-size
   pieces

Ground Ingredients
12 shallots
3 cloves garlic
1¼ cm (½ in) ginger
1 tablespoon coriander
2 tablespoons fennel
1 tablespoon poppy seeds

180 g (6 oz) or ½ bottle tomato sauce
1 large can (410 g/15 oz) evaporated milk
15 shallots, sliced, fried crisp and
   crushed lightly
6 tablespoons oil
1 onion, sliced

2½ cm (1 in) stick cinnamon
5 cardamoms
5 cloves
2 screwpine leaves, knotted
2 teaspoons salt

Marinate chicken with ground ingredients, tomato sauce, evaporated milk and shallot crisps. Leave aside for 30 minutes.

Heat oil in a *kuali* and fry onion and spices until fragrant. Put in marinated chicken and bring to a slow boil. Add screwpine leaves and salt and simmer over low heat for 25 minutes or until chicken is tender.

Rojak Betik Trengganu

Preparation: 30 minutes   Cooking: 10 minutes

½ small half-ripe papaya, shredded
240 g (8 oz) beansprouts, scalded
½ pineapple, quartered and sliced
½ cucumber, halved and sliced

Sauce
3 mackerels,
    grilled and flaked
20 dried chillies, soaked   } *ground*
1¼ x 2½ cm (½ x 1 in)
    dried shrimp paste
60 g (2 oz) palm sugar
1 cup water
1 tablespoon tamarind paste
1 dessertspoon vinegar
1 teaspoon salt

Combine shredded papaya and beansprouts and place in a dish. Top with pineapple and cucumber slices. Leave aside.

Sauce
Put ground ingredients into a mixing bowl.

Place palm sugar and water in a saucepan and boil over low heat until sugar dissolves. Add tamarind paste, mix well and strain. Pour over ground ingredients and blend with vinegar and salt to taste.

Just before serving, pour sauce over prepared vegetables.

Nasi Minyak

Preparation: 15 minutes   Cooking: 25 minutes

450 g (1 lb) rice
4 tablespoons ghee
6 shallots |
2 cloves garlic | *sliced*
1¼ cm (½ in) ginger, shredded
2½ cm (1 in) stick cinnamon
3 cloves
3 cardamoms
2 sections of a star anise
2³/₄ cups water
3 screwpine leaves, knotted
3 tablespoons evaporated milk
1 heaped teaspoon salt
90 g (3 oz) raisins
shallot crisps

Wash rice, drain and put into a rice cooker.

Heat ghee in a *kuali* and fry shallots, garlic, ginger and spices until fragrant. Add water, screwpine leaves, evaporated milk and salt. Stir well and bring to a boil. Pour contents of *kuali* into rice cooker. Cook till rice is done.

Serve hot sprinkled with raisins and shallot crisps.

Nasi Ulam

Preparation: 30 minutes   Cooking: 30 minutes

Sambal Ingredients
1 coconut, grated (for 1 cup thick
   coconut milk)
10 red chillies ⎫
5 shallots ⎬ *ground*
1¼ cm (½ in) ginger ⎭
1 stalk lemon grass, crushed lightly
¼ teaspoon salt
1 teaspoon tamarind paste ⎫ *mixed and*
2 tablespoons water ⎬ *strained*

3 mackerels, grilled,
   flaked and ground

Ingredients to be Sliced Finely
5 turmeric leaves
4 sprigs polygonum
4 stalks basil
5 stalks 'selasih' leaves
4 stalks watercress
3 'cekur' leaves
3 double lime leaves
3 lettuce leaves
4 cashewnut leaves
2 stalks lemon grass (use only the
   tender central portion)
6 shallots
1 wild ginger flower
3 green chillies

½ white coconut, grated for 'kerisik'
juice of 1 large lime
1 teaspoon salt
sufficient cooked rice for 8 persons

Sambal
Put thick coconut milk together with ground ingredients, lemon grass, salt and tamarind juice in a pot and simmer over low heat, stirring frequently, until sauce is thick and oil separates.

Preparing and Serving Nasi Ulam
Combine ground fish with all the finely sliced ingredients and *kerisik*.

Heat a *kuali* without adding oil until it is hot. Turn off heat, put in combined ingredients, lime juice and salt and mix well. Place on a serving dish.

To serve Nasi Ulam, ladle a portion of rice onto a plate, top with required amount of combined ingredients and *sambal*. Mix well.

Kuih Belimbing

Preparation: 15 minutes   Cooking: 20 minutes   Makes: 40

Pastry
150 g (5 oz) flour
pinch of salt
60 g (2 oz) butter
³/₄ cup water
2 eggs
½ teaspoon vanilla essence

Syrup
120 g (4 oz) sugar
1 cup water

Pastry
Sift flour into a mixing bowl and add salt. Heat butter and water together in a small saucepan, bring to a boil and pour immediately into flour.

Beat until paste forms a ball. Cool slightly, then beat in eggs and vanilla essence. The mixture should be a little stiff and hold its shape when piped.

Fit a cookie press with a star nozzle and pipe 5 cm (2 in) lengths of the mixture into hot oil. Stir Kuih Belimbing as they float up to brown evenly. Drain on absorbent paper. Arrange on a dish and just before serving pour syrup over.

Syrup
Place sugar and water in a small saucepan and bring to a boil. Cool before pouring over Kuih Belimbing.

Sri Kaya Peringi

Preparation: 30 minutes   Cooking: 40 minutes

1 medium pumpkin, approx. 3 kg (6⅔ lb) and
    about 23-25½ cm (9-10 in) in diameter
300 g (10 oz) palm sugar, chopped finely
¼ cup water
7 eggs
1½ coconuts, grated (for 1³/₄ cups
    'pati santan')
1 dessertspoon screwpine juice

Wash pumpkin and carefully cut a 10-12½ cm (4-5 in) circle from the top. Using a spoon, remove seed and soft portion to leave a hollow case. Skin top circle. Cut pumpkin (from both hollow and top circle) into neat 1¼ cm (½ in) cubes. Place pumpkin cubes into pumpkin case.

Place chopped palm sugar and water in a small saucepan and cook over low heat, stirring until sugar dissolves. Strain.

In a mixing bowl, stir eggs lightly with coconut milk. Add screwpine juice and palm sugar syrup. Mix well.

Strain egg mixture into pumpkin case. Stir mixture, then place pumpkin case in a large steamer. Steam for 35-40 minutes until pumpkin is cooked.

Serve soft custard hot or cold in small bowls.

PENANG

Penang is very often referred to as the Pearl of the Orient. This exotic sun-splashed island boasts some of the finest beaches in Malaysia. One of the former British Straits Settlements, Penang was a prosperous trading post and entrepot centre and its population became very cosmopolitan with indigenous Malays and an influx of migrant Chinese, Indians and Arabs.

Malay curries show an Indian influence, though they are not as pungent as authentic Indian curries. There are local preparations of Kurma, Dalca and crab curries. There is also Gulai Masri which hints of an Arabic influence.

Highly popular Nonya food, a delicious hybrid of Chinese and Malay cuisines, has its own flavours owing to the frequent use of ginger, galingale, lemon grass and dried shrimp paste. The Nonyas love a sour tang to their food and this is provided by the juice of tamarind paste, dried tamarind skin or tiny acidic fruit called *belimbing buluh*. Nonya favourites are Penang Laksa, Penang Acar, Curry Kapitan, Roti Jala, Otak Otak and a host of enticing curries.

Opposite: Otak Otak Pulau Pinang

Otak Otak Pulau Pinang

(photograph on page 144)

Preparation: 25 minutes   Cooking: 20 minutes   Makes: 20 packets

1 kg (2¹/₅ lb) threadfin, central portion
1 teaspoon salt
6 eggs

Ground Ingredients
10 dried chillies, soaked
8 shallots
3 cloves garlic
4 stalks lemon grass
4 slices galingale
2½ cm (1 in) turmeric root
1¼ cm (½ in) square dried shrimp paste
6 candlenuts
3 dessertspoons coriander
36 peppercorns

3 teaspoons salt
16 double lime leaves, sliced finely
1½ coconuts (for 1¼ cups 'pati santan')
banana leaves
20 'kaduk' leaves

Wash and cut fish into two halves, then cut into 5 x 4 cm (2 x 1½ in) pieces. Season fish with salt and leave for 15 minutes.

Lightly beat eggs with a fork and stir in ground ingredients, salt and sliced double lime leaves. Mix with *pati santan*.

Run banana leaves over heat until softened, then cut into 15 x 18 cm (6 x 7 in) pieces. Make sure there are no holes or slits in the leaves or gravy will seep through. Wash and dry the leaves.

Put a *kaduk* leaf and fish in the centre of a banana leaf. Fold as shown in Otak Otak Tenggiri (page 4) and fasten with a satay stick. Trim the top neatly with scissors and steam for 20 minutes.

Indian Fish Curry

(photograph opposite)

Preparation: 15 minutes   Cooking: 20 minutes

600 g (1⅓ lb) black pomfret,
    cut into two portions
1 teaspoon salt
¾ cup oil
25 dried chillies, soaked ⎤
240 g (8 oz) shallots   ⎬ ground
4 stalks lemon grass   ⎦
4 tablespoons fish curry powder ⎤ combined
½ cup water   ⎦
1 teaspoon mustard seeds
1 dessertspoon tamarind paste ⎤ mixed and
3 tablespoons water   ⎦ strained
1 onion, sliced into rings
3 stalks curry leaves
1 coconut, grated (for 1 cup thick coconut
    milk and 2 cups thin coconut milk)
2-3 eggplants, sliced at a slant
1 teaspoon salt
3 tomatoes, quartered

Rub fish with salt and leave aside.

Heat oil in a *kuali* and fry ground ingredients until fragrant. Add curry powder paste and mustard seeds and fry until fragrant. To prevent mixture from sticking to pan add a little tamarind juice.

Put in onion and curry leaves and fry for 3 minutes. Add remaining tamarind juice, and thin coconut milk. When it comes to a boil add eggplants. Simmer over low heat until soft. Pour in thick coconut milk. When it boils again put in fish, salt and tomatoes and simmer till fish is cooked.

Opposite: Indian Fish Curry

Indian Fish Curry with Bittergourd

Preparation: 15 minutes Cooking: 15 minutes

1 medium black pomfret,
   cut into slices
1 teaspoon salt
4 tablespoons oil
5 cloves garlic, sliced
2 onions, sliced
3 stalks curry leaves
1 teaspoon fenugreek
2½ cm (1 in) ginger   ⎱ ground
2½ cm (1 in) turmeric root ⎰
2 heaped tablespoons
   fish curry powder   ⎱ combined
¼ cup water   ⎰
2 tablespoons tamarind paste ⎱ mixed and
4 tablespoons water   ⎰ strained
1 coconut, grated (for 1 cup thick
   coconut milk and 3 cups thin
   coconut milk)
1 bittergourd, seed portions scraped off,
   cut into 4 cm (1½ in) pieces, soaked in
   salt water
1 teaspoon salt
1 teaspoon sugar

Season fish with salt and leave for 15 minutes.

Heat oil in a *kuali* and brown garlic and onions. Add curry leaves, fenugreek and ground ingredients and fry for a few minutes. Add curry powder paste and fry until fragrant. Put in tamarind juice and thin coconut milk and bring to a boil.

Add bittergourd and simmer for 5 minutes then put in fish. Simmer until fish is cooked and bittergourd is tender. Pour in thick coconut milk and add salt and sugar to taste.

Udang Tumis Petai

(photograph opposite)

Preparation: 30 minutes   Cooking: 15 minutes

15 pods 'petai'
6 tablespoons oil
2½ cm (1 in) galingale   ⎫
2½ cm (1 in) turmeric root   ⎬ ground
10 roasted cashew nuts   ⎪ ingredients 'A'
4 stalks lemon grass   ⎭
20 dried chillies, soaked   ⎫
5 red chillies   ⎪
5 bird chillies   ⎪
240 g (8 oz) shallots   ⎬ ground
2 cloves garlic   ⎪ ingredients 'B'
4 x 2½ cm (1½ x 1 in)   ⎪
   dried shrimp paste   ⎭
600 g (1⅓ lb) small
   prawns, shelled

1 heaped tablespoon tamarind paste ⎱ mixed and
½ cup water   ⎰ strained
1 teaspoon sugar
1½ teaspoons salt

Remove *petai* from pods and peel off outer skin. Heat oil in a *kuali* and fry ground ingredients 'A' until fragrant. Add ground ingredients 'B' and fry over low heat until fragrant and oil separates.

Put in prawns and stir-fry for a few minutes, taking care not to overcook prawns. Add tamarind juice and bring to a slow boil. Put in *petai*, stir in sugar and salt and stir-fry for 2 minutes.

Opposite: Udang Tumis Petai and Ayam Tumis

Crab Curry

Preparation: 30 minutes   Cooking: 25 minutes

1½ kg (3⅓ lb) crabs
½ medium pineapple
6 tablespoons oil
6 shallots, sliced
3 cloves garlic, sliced
1 tablespoon chilli powder
2 tablespoons coriander
    powder
1 teaspoon turmeric
    powder

} *mixed to a paste with water*

Ground Ingredients
8 shallots
4 cloves garlic
2½ cm (1 in) ginger
3 cardamoms
2 sections of a star anise
1¼ cm (½ in) stick cinnamon
2 cloves
1 heaped teaspoon poppy seeds
½ teaspoon black peppercorns
½ white coconut, grated for 'kerisik'

½ coconut, grated (for 1¼ cups
    coconut milk)
1 teaspoon salt

Clean crabs and remove and crack pincers with a pestle. Trim legs and cut each crab into four pieces.

Halve pineapple lengthwise and cut into 2½ cm (½ in) slices.

Heat oil in a *kuali* and lightly brown shallots and garlic. Put in chilli paste mixture and fry for a few minutes. Add ground ingredients and fry until fragrant, adding a little coconut milk to prevent ingredients from sticking to pan.

Put in crabs and stir-fry for a few minutes until well coated with ground ingredients. Add coconut milk and bring to a boil. Lower heat and put in pineapple and salt to taste. Simmer for a few minutes until crabs are cooked and very little gravy remains.

Dalca

Preparation: 25 minutes   Cooking: 1 ¼ hours

600 g (1 ⅓ lb) beef, with bones
3 heaped tablespoons meat curry powder
2½ cm (1 in) stick cinnamon
3 cardamoms
2 sections of a star anise
2 teaspoons salt
1 coconut, grated (for 1 cup thick
   coconut milk and 3 cups thin
   coconut milk)
300 g (10 oz) potatoes, cut into wedges
3 eggplants, cut into 1¼ cm (½ in) slices
2 tablespoons tamarind paste | *mixed and*
5 tablespoons water | *strained*
½ cup lentils
3 tomatoes, quartered
4 green chillies
3 tablespoons oil
6 shallots |
2½ cm (1 in) ginger | *sliced*

Cut beef into 4 cm (1½ in) cubes.

Put beef, curry powder, spices, salt and thin coconut milk into an earthen pot and bring to a slow boil.

Lower heat and simmer for 40 minutes until beef is tender. Add potatoes and simmer for 10 minutes then add eggplants and simmer till almost soft.

Add thick coconut milk, tamarind juice and lentils. When it comes to a boil, put in tomatoes and green chillies. Cook for 3 minutes then remove from heat.

Heat 3 tablespoons oil in a *kuali* and brown shallots and ginger. Pour over Dalca and stir to mix well.

Serve with rice or *roti canai*.

Kurma

Preparation: 20 minutes Cooking: (Beef) ¾ -1 hour (Chicken) 30 minutes

1 kg (2¹⁄₅ lb) beef or 1½ kg (3⅓ lb) chicken
4 tablespoons ghee
10 shallots | *sliced*
3 cloves garlic |
2½ cm (1 in) stick cinnamon
4 cardamoms
4 tablespoons kurma curry powder,
   mixed to a paste with a little water
1½ teaspoons salt
1 coconut, grated (for 3 cups
   coconut milk)
2 heaped tablespoons powdered milk | *combined*
½ cup water |
juice of 1 large lime
2 onions, slit across as in diagram
   on page 106
4 sprigs mint leaves

Cut beef into small pieces. If using chicken, cut into bite-size pieces.

Heat ghee in an earthen pot and fry shallots, garlic and spices until fragrant. Add curry powder paste and fry over low heat until fragrant.

Put in meat, add salt and cook over low heat until meat is almost tender, adding a little coconut milk to prevent meat from sticking to pot. Pour in remaining coconut milk and bring to a boil.

Combine milk mixture and lime juice and add to Kurma. When it boils again put in onions and simmer over low heat for 20 minutes until meat is tender and oil appears on surface.

Add mint leaves just before removing from heat.

Kari Kambing

Preparation: 20 minutes   Cooking: 30 minutes

600 g (1⅓ lb) mutton, cut into
   2½ cm (1 in) cubes
6 tablespoons oil
12 shallots
5 cloves garlic   } *sliced*
4 cm (1½ in) ginger
1 stalk curry leaves
5 cm (2 in) stick cinnamon
1 whole star anise
2 cardamoms
4 cloves
½ coconut, grated (for 1 cup thick
   coconut milk and 1½ cups thin
   coconut milk)
2 tablespoons meat curry powder
½ tablespoon fennel powder
3 potatoes, quartered and fried
juice of ½ large lime
2 teaspoons salt

Cut mutton into 2½ cm (1 in) cubes.

Heat oil in a pressure cooker and brown sliced ingredients and curry leaves. Put in spices and fry until fragrant. Add mutton and fry for a few minutes, then put in thin coconut milk. Cover and pressure cook for 10 minutes.

At the end of that time add thick coconut milk and when it comes to a boil, stir in curry and fennel powder. If a thicker curry is preferred, simmer over low heat for 5 minutes then put in potatoes and simmer till cooked. Stir in lime juice and salt before removing from heat.

Rendang Daging

Preparation: 20 minutes   Cooking: 1½ hours

1 kg (2⅕ lb) beef
1 cup oil

Ground Ingredients
300 g (10 oz) shallots, ground coarsely,
   separately
40 dried chillies, soaked and seeded
5 red chillies, seeded
4 cloves garlic
2½ cm (1 in) ginger
4 cm (1½ in) turmeric root
2 stalks lemon grass
10 untoasted cashew nuts

2 stalks lemon grass, crushed lightly
2 tablespoons meat curry powder
1 coconut, grated (for ½ cup 'pati santan'
   and 2½ cups thin coconut milk)
2 heaped teaspoons salt

Cut meat across the grain into thin 4 cm (1½ in) slices.

Heat oil in a *kuali* and fry shallots for 5 minutes until lightly browned. Add remaining ground ingredients and crushed lemon grass. Fry over low heat until fragrant. Mix curry powder with a little of the thin coconut milk, add to ground ingredients and continue frying until oil separates. If necessary, add more of the thin coconut milk to prevent mixture from sticking to pan.

Put in beef and fry until water from meat evaporates, then pour in remaining thin coconut milk. Simmer until thick, stirring occasionally.

Put in *pati santan* and salt to taste. Continue cooking, stirring all the time to prevent ingredients from sticking to pan, until gravy is thick and meat is tender. Serve with rice.

Ayam Tumis

(photograph on page 149)

Preparation: 25 minutes   Cooking: 30 minutes

1 chicken (1½ kg/3⅓ lb)
¾ cup oil
2 wild ginger flowers, sliced finely
2 stalks lemon grass, crushed

Ground Ingredients
35-40 dried chillies, soaked
5 x 2½ cm (2 x 1 in) dried shrimp paste
4 stalks lemon grass
6 cloves garlic
10 slices galingale
4 cm (1½ in) turmeric root
240 g (8 oz) shallots

2 tablespoons tamarind paste ⎱ *mixed and*
3 cups water ⎰ *strained*
1 tablespoon sugar
½ teaspoon monosodium glutamate
2 teaspoons salt

Cut chicken into serving-size pieces.

Heat oil in a *kuali* and fry wild ginger flowers and lemon grass for 1-2 minutes, then add ground ingredients and fry till fragrant. Put in chicken pieces. Stir-fry till well coated with ground ingredients.

Add tamarind juice and bring to a boil. Add sugar, monosodium glutamate and salt. Lower heat and allow to simmer for 15-20 minutes until chicken is tender.

Serve with rice.

Curry Kapitan

Preparation: 20 minutes   Cooking: 40 minutes

1½ kg (3⅓ lb) chicken
4 tablespoons oil
2 onions, diced
2 teaspoons salt

Ground Ingredients
15 red chillies
15 shallots
4 cloves garlic
2½ cm (1 in) turmeric root
10 candlenuts
5 x 2½ cm (2 x 1 in) dried shrimp paste
4 stalks lemon grass

1 coconut, grated (for 1 cup thick coconut milk and 3 cups thin coconut milk)
juice of 1 or 2 large limes

Cut chicken into bite-size pieces.

Heat oil in a *kuali* and lightly brown onions with salt. Add ground ingredients and fry till fragrant, adding a little of the thick coconut milk to prevent ingredients from sticking to pan.

Add chicken and fry for a few minutes. Pour thin coconut milk over chicken and cook over low heat until chicken is tender, then add remaining thick coconut milk. When curry boils, add the lime juice.

Serve Curry Kapitan with rice or Roti Jala (page 160).

Kari Ayam Kering

Preparation: 20 minutes   Cooking: 35 minutes

**1 kg (2¹/₅ lb) chicken, cut into
  bite-size pieces**
1 teaspoon salt
2 tablespoons meat curry powder

Ground Ingredients
8 red chillies
8 shallots
2 cloves garlic
3 slices ginger
3 cloves
8 cardamoms

8 tablespoons oil
2 onions, sliced
**3 potatoes, quartered and soaked in
  salt water**
**1 coconut, grated (for 1 cup thick coconut
  milk and 1½ cups thin coconut milk)**
2 stalks curry leaves
1 teaspoon salt

Marinate chicken with salt, curry powder and ground ingredients and leave for 30 minutes.

Heat oil in a *kuali* and fry sliced onions until transparent and fragrant. Drain from oil and leave aside. Put in drained potatoes and fry for 5 minutes until lightly browned. Drain and keep aside.

Put in seasoned chicken and fry for 10 minutes, add thin coconut milk and curry leaves and bring to a boil. Simmer gently until chicken is almost tender, then put in fried potatoes, salt and thick coconut milk. Cook over low heat, stirring frequently, until chicken is tender and gravy dry.

Serve garnished with fried sliced onions.

Ayam Masak Cabai

Preparation: 20 minutes   Cooking: 35 minutes

**1½ kg (3⅓ lb) chicken, cut into
  serving-size pieces**
300 g (10 oz) red chillies, seeded ⎫
2½ cm (1 in) ginger   ⎬ ground
2 onions   ⎭
2 pieces dried tamarind skin
**1 coconut, grated (for 3 cups
  coconut milk)**
**½ can (285 g/9½ oz) condensed tomato
  soup**
3 tomatoes, quartered
1½ teaspoons salt
4 sprigs mint leaves

Put chicken, ground ingredients, dried tamarind skin, coconut milk and tomato soup into an earthen pot and bring to a slow boil.

Lower heat and simmer over low heat for 30 minutes, stirring frequently until chicken is tender and oil appears on surface. Add tomatoes and salt and cook for 2 minutes. Just before removing from heat throw in mint leaves.

Encik Kebin

Preparation: 10 minutes   Cooking: 10 minutes

**1½ kg (3⅓ lb) chicken, cut into
5 cm (2 in) pieces**

Ground Ingredients
15 dried chillies, soaked
1 tablespoon coriander
2 teaspoons fennel
1 teaspoon cummin
1¼ cm (½ in) stick cinnamon
2 cloves
1 teaspoon pepper
½ teaspoon turmeric powder

1 teaspoon ginger juice
1½ teaspoons salt
**½ coconut, grated (for ½ cup
'pati santan')**
oil for deep-frying
cucumber slices
tomato slices

Wash chicken and wipe dry.

Marinate chicken with ground ingredients, ginger juice, salt and *pati santan* and leave for at least 1 hour.

Heat oil in a *kuali* till smoking hot. Put in chicken and deep-fry without stirring for 2 minutes. Lower heat and cook till golden brown.

Remove to a plate, garnished with cucumber and tomato slices.

Penang Rojak

Preparation: 20 minutes   Cooking: 10 minutes

Rojak Sauce
25 dried chillies, soaked
**2½ cm (1 in) square dried shrimp
paste, toasted** } *ground*
4 heaped tablespoons tamarind paste | *mixed and*
½ cup water | *strained*
5 tablespoons sugar
1 teaspoon dark soy sauce

1 cucumber
2 small green mangoes, skinned
½ medium pineapple
300 g (10 oz) turnip
3 teaspoons black shrimp paste
**150 g (5 oz) peanut candy or roasted
peanuts, ground coarsely**
1 tablespoon roasted sesame seeds

Put ground ingredients and tamarind juice in a small saucepan and cook over low heat. Stir in sugar and dark soy sauce and cook until sugar dissolves and sauce is thick. Let it cool.

Cut cucumber, mangoes, pineapple and turnip, in small wedges, into a large mixing bowl. Put in cooled Rojak sauce and black shrimp paste and mix well.

Add ground peanut candy and roasted sesame seeds. Stir well and serve immediately.

Penang Acar

(photograph opposite)

Preparation: 45 minutes   Cooking: 20 minutes

1¼ kg (2¾ lb) cucumbers,
    halved lengthwise, soft portions
    removed, cut into 4 cm (1½ in) strips
1 carrot, scraped and cut into
    4 cm (1½ in) strips
1 tablespoon salt
1½ cups vinegar
300 g (10 oz) long beans, cut into
    4 cm (1½ in) lengths
600 g (1⅓ lb) cabbage, cut into 2½ cm
    (1 in) pieces
4 red chillies, halved lengthwise,
    seeded and cut into thin strips
2 cups oil

Ground Ingredients

20 dried chillies, soaked } *ground*
6 red chillies   } *separately*
360 g (12 oz) shallots
1 whole pod garlic
2½ cm (1 in) turmeric root
2½ cm (1 in) galingale
3 candlenuts

180 g (6 oz) sugar
1 teaspoon salt
600 g (1⅓ lb) peanuts, roasted and
    ground coarsely

Put cucumber and carrot strips in a bowl and mix well with salt. Leave for 30 minutes, then wash thoroughly with water. Drain. Put cucumber and carrot strips in a piece of muslin cloth a little at a time and squeeze out as much water as possible.

Boil half a large saucepan of water with ¾ cup of the vinegar. When it comes to a boil, put in all the vegetables including cucumber and carrot strips.

Immediately pour vegetables into a colander and drain well. Put vegetables in the sun to dry for 30 minutes.

Heat oil in a *kuali* and fry ground chillies for 2 minutes, then add remaining ground ingredients and fry until fragrant and oil separates. Add remaining vinegar, then sugar and salt. Stir in coarsely ground peanuts and mix thoroughly.

Add to vegetables and mix well. Keep Acar aside for 3 hours before serving.

Opposite: Penang Acar

Nasi Kunyit

Preparation: 15 minutes   Cooking: 1¼ hours

1¼ kg (2³/₄ lb) glutinous rice
4 large pieces dried turmeric root
1 teaspoon salt
banana leaves
2½ coconuts, grated (for 2 cups
    'pati santan')
½ teaspoon salt

Wash rice. Crush turmeric and wrap in a piece of clean cloth. Soak rice overnight with turmeric and salt.

The next day, line base of a shallow bamboo basket with banana leaves. Put rice in the basket and place in a steamer. Steam for 1 hour till rice is cooked and soft.

Dish out cooked rice into a heatproof dish or pot and pour in coconut milk mixed with salt, stirring well with a spoon at the same time. Return rice to steamer and steam for a further 10-15 minutes.

Dish out rice onto a plate and lightly press into a mould with a spoon.

Serve with any chicken curry.

Chicken Biryani

Preparation: 20 minutes   Cooking: 40 minutes

4 tablespoons ghee
2 sticks cinnamon, each 9 cm
    (3½ in) long
3 whole star anise
5 onions, sliced
1½ kg (3⅓ lb) chicken, cut into 6
    large pieces
1 dessertspoon turmeric powder
1¼ cm (½ in) ginger ⎫
3 cloves garlic ⎪
8 shallots ⎬ ground together
1 teaspoon chilli powder ⎪
1 teaspoon black peppercorns ⎭
½ cup yoghurt
4 tomatoes, quartered
4 green chillies, kept whole
1 tablespoon salt
3 stalks curry leaves
½ coconut, grated (for 3½ cups
    coconut milk)
1 tablespoon ground almonds
1 tablespoon ground cashew nuts

2 cups Basmati (long-grain) rice,
    washed and drained
3 screwpine leaves, knotted

Heat ghee in a pan and fry spices for a minute, then lightly brown onions. Add chicken and fry well, then add turmeric powder and ground ingredients. Put in yoghurt, tomatoes, green chillies, salt and curry leaves and simmer gently for a few minutes.

Pour in half the coconut milk and stir in ground almonds and cashew nuts. Bring to a boil, then add remaining coconut milk.

Put well-drained rice and chicken curry mixture into a pot or rice cooker to finish cooking. Halfway through cooking, add screwpine leaves and stir well.

Serve hot, each serving with a portion of chicken.

Penang Laksa

Preparation: 1½ hours   Cooking: 30 minutes

4 tablespoons tamarind paste } *mixed and*
1 cup water } *strained*

Ground Ingredients
40 dried chillies, soaked
6 slices galingale
1¼ x 2½ x 5 cm (½ x 1 x 2 in)
  dried shrimp paste
3 stalks lemon grass
180 g (6 oz) shallots

6 cups water
10-12 sprigs polygonum leaves
3-4 wild ginger flowers, buds split
  and stems smashed
4 pieces dried tamarind skin
1³/₄ kg (4 lb) wolf herring,
  steamed and flaked
2 tablespoons sugar
salt to taste
600 g (1⅓ lb) fresh thick rice vermicelli
  parboiled

Garnishing Ingredients
½ pineapple, sliced and cut into
  strips
1 cucumber, skinned and shredded
½ head lettuce, shredded finely
1 onion, sliced finely
3 red chillies, seeded and sliced
1 sprig mint leaves
6-8 small limes, halved
black shrimp paste,
  mixed with a little water

Put tamarind juice, ground ingredients and water to boil in an earthen pot. Add polygonum leaves, wild ginger flowers and dried tamarind skin and simmer over low heat for 15 minutes.

Add flaked fish, sugar and salt to taste. Simmer for a few minutes. Remove polygonum leaves, wild ginger flowers and dried tamarind skin just before dishing out gravy.

To serve, put some noodles in individual bowls and garnish with a little of each garnishing ingredient. Pour boiling gravy over noodles and add 1 teaspoon black shrimp paste. Serve immediately.

Roti Jala (Lacy Pancake)

Preparation: 15 minutes   Cooking: 30 minutes   Makes: 24

2 cups flour
½ teaspoon salt
2 eggs, beaten
½ white coconut, grated (for 2½ cups coconut milk)

Sift flour into a bowl and add salt. Stir in beaten eggs and coconut milk and beat until smooth. Strain batter if it is lumpy.

Grease and heat a non-stick pan over low heat. Put a ladleful of batter into Roti Jala cup with four funnels and move it in a circular motion over pan so that pancake will have a lacy pattern. Cook until set. Turn over onto a dish. Continue frying pancakes until batter is used up.

When cool, fold pancakes into two or fold once and roll up. Serve with Curry Kapitan or your favourite curry.

Kuih Ko Swee

(photograph opposite)

Preparation: 15 minutes   Cooking: 25 minutes

180 g (6 oz) palm sugar, chopped
60 g (2 oz) sugar
1 cup water
2 screwpine leaves, knotted
150 g (5 oz) wet rice flour ⎫
120 g (4 oz) sago flour ⎪
1 cup water ⎬ *'A'*
⅛ teaspoon lime paste ⎪
1 teaspoon alkaline water ⎭
150 g (5 oz) dry rice flour ⎫
60 g (2 oz) sago flour ⎪
1½ cups water ⎬ *'B'*
⅛ teaspoon borax ('pangsar') ⎪
1 teaspoon alkaline water ⎭
150 g (5 oz) white grated coconut, from a young coconut
pinch of salt

Put palm sugar, sugar, water and screwpine leaves in a saucepan and bring to a slow boil to dissolve sugar.

Use either ingredients 'A' or 'B'. If using 'A' blend wet rice flour, sago flour, water, lime paste and alkaline water in a bowl till smooth. Strain hot boiled syrup gradually into the flour mixture, stirring till well mixed. If using 'B' sift rice flour and sago flour into a mixing bowl. Add water and mix till smooth. Strain syrup gradually into flour mixture, stirring till well mixed, then stir in borax and alkaline water.

Steam 22 small Chinese teacups for 5 minutes. Stir flour mixture thoroughly, then fill cups. For easier filling, pour mixture into a large measuring jug with a beak. There should be approximately 3 cups of flour mixture.

Steam over moderate heat for 20 minutes. Cool, remove from cups and roll in grated coconut mixed with salt.

Opposite: Kuih Ko Swee

KEDAH

Kedah, rice bowl of Malaysia, is situated in the north of Peninsular Malaysia. As far as the eye can see are stretches of flat padi fields and in the harvesting season the rich golden fields are a bustle of activity.

Malay cuisine is a delicious reflection of cooking styles in the north. Laksa Kedah, tangy sour with flaked fish, is good 'n' *pedas*. Dalca Daging Kedah is a vegetable curry given added flavour with beef bones. The Arabian influence in Acar Limau and Masak Arab Daging makes them deliciously different.

Opposite: Opor Ayam

Panggang Ikan Terubuk

Preparation: 10 minutes   Grilling: 15 minutes

**1 medium shad, cleaned, but with
  scales left on**

Ground Ingredients
2 red chillies
6 bird chillies
1 stalk lemon grass
6 shallots
2½ cm (1 in) turmeric root
1 tablespoon grated coconut
2 teaspoons salt

Marinate fish with ground ingredients and leave for 30 minutes.

Grill over glowing charcoal on both sides for approximately 15 minutes or until cooked.

Remove scales and serve hot with boiled white rice.

Masak Asam Ikan Kerapu

Preparation: 10 minutes   Cooking: 15 minutes

3 slices grouper or black pomfret
1 teaspoon salt
2½ cm (1 in) turmeric root, ground
3 tablespoons oil
½ coconut, grated (for 1½ cups coconut milk)
3 red chillies, seeded and sliced
2 slices ginger, cut into strips
3 shallots, sliced
3 cloves garlic, sliced
2 pieces dried tamarind skin
½ teaspoon salt

Season fish with salt and ground turmeric and leave aside. Heat oil in a *kuali* until hot and fry fish for 2 minutes on each side. Dish out.

Put coconut milk and remaining ingredients into a pot and bring to a slow boil. Allow to simmer for 5 minutes over low heat. Add fried fish slices and boil for 2 minutes.

Masak Arab Daging

Preparation: 20 minutes   Cooking: 1 hour

1 kg (2¹/₅ lb) beef, cut into thin 5 cm (2 in)
   slices

Ground Ingredients
300 g (10 oz) ripe tomatoes
300 g (10 oz) shallots
90 g (3 oz) sesame seeds
½ teaspoon fennel
½ teaspoon cummin
½ teaspoon pepper
1¼ cm (½ in) ginger
2½ cm (1 in) turmeric root

4 tablespoons oil
6 shallots, sliced
4 cloves garlic, sliced
1 coconut, grated (for 4 cups coconut
   milk)

1 small can (70 g/2 oz) tomato puree
1½ teaspoons salt

Marinate beef with ground ingredients and leave
for 1 hour.

Heat 4 tablespoons oil in a *kuali* and brown shallots and garlic. Put in marinated meat and fry
gently till water evaporates. Add coconut milk
and stir until it comes to a boil. Lower heat and
simmer gently, stirring frequently until gravy is
thick and meat is tender. Add tomato puree and
simmer for 5 minutes, stirring continuously. Add
salt to taste.

Serunding Daging, Kedah Style

(photograph on page 169)

Preparation: 30 minutes   Cooking: 2 hours

300 g (10 oz) beef

Ground Ingredients
15 dried chillies, soaked
10 shallots
2 cloves garlic
2 stalks lemon grass
2½ cm (1 in) galingale
1¼ cm (½ in) ginger
2½ cm (1 in) square dried shrimp paste
2 tablespoons coriander
1 teaspoon cummin

2 double lime leaves, sliced finely
1 turmeric leaf, sliced finely
1 heaped teaspoon tamarind paste ⎫ *mixed and*
3 tablespoons water   ⎬ *strained*
1 tablespoon sugar   ⎭
½ coconut, grated (for 1 cup
   coconut milk)
½ white coconut, grated,
   dry-roasted till light brown
1½ teaspoons salt

Simmer beef in a saucepan for 1 hour with enough
water to cover meat, or put in a pressure cooker
and pressure cook for 30 minutes. Remove and
drain in a colander until dry and cool. Cut into 2½
cm (1 in) cubes, then break meat with fingers into
small pieces.

Marinate meat with ground ingredients, double
lime leaves, turmeric leaf, tamarind juice and
sugar and leave for 15 minutes.

Put marinated meat and coconut milk in a *kuali*
and bring to a slow boil. Lower heat and fry continuously until almost dry, then add coconut and
salt to taste. Cook for a further 30 minutes on very
low heat, stirring all the time until completely dry.

Dalca Daging Kedah

Preparation: 25 minutes   Cooking: 35 minutes

300 g (10 oz) beef, with or without bones,
   cut into 2½ cm (1 in) pieces
½ white coconut, grated for 'kerisik'
4 tablespoons oil

Ground Ingredients
15 dried chillies, soaked
2 teaspoons coriander
½ teaspoon fennel
½ teaspoon cummin
6 mm (¼ in) stick cinnamon
1 clove
1 section of a star anise
½ teaspoon black peppercorns
½ teaspoon turmeric powder

½ coconut, grated (for 3 cups coconut
   milk)
1 eggplant, cut at a slant into 2½ cm (1 in)
   slices
5 long beans, cut into 5 cm (2 in) lengths
2 red chillies, seeded and split
4 small sour starfruit, halved lengthwise

2 potatoes, cut into 2 cm (³/₄ in)
   cubes and fried
2 tomatoes, quartered
2 teaspoons salt

Marinate beef with *kerisik* and leave for 15 minutes.

Heat oil in a pot and fry ground ingredients until fragrant and oil separates. Add meat and fry for 5 minutes. Put in coconut milk and bring to a boil. Add eggplant, long beans, chillies, small sour starfruit, and potatoes. Simmer over low heat until vegetables are tender. Put in tomatoes and add salt to taste.

Opor Ayam

(photograph on page 162)

Preparation: 15 minutes   Cooking: 30 minutes

5 tablespoons oil

Ground Ingredients
12 shallots
4 cloves garlic
2½ cm (1 in) ginger
2½ cm (1 in) galingale
2 stalks lemon grass
1 tablespoon coriander
1 teaspoon white peppercorns
10 candlenuts

1½ kg (3⅓ lb) chicken, cut into bite-size
   pieces
1 coconut, grated (for 3 cups coconut
   milk)
2 teaspoons salt

Heat oil in a *kuali* and fry ground ingredients over low heat until fragrant and oil separates.

Add chicken, fry well for 3 minutes then pour in coconut milk. Bring to a slow boil, lower heat and simmer for 20 minutes or until chicken is tender. Add 2 teaspoons salt or to taste.

Serve Opor Ayam with white boiled rice.

Note: Three daun salam *may be added, if available, to give fragrance.*

Acar Limau

Preparation: 20 minutes   Cooking: 25 minutes

8 tablespoons oil

Ground Ingredients
5 shallots
4 cloves garlic
7 cloves
2 sections of a star anise
5 cm (2 in) stick cinnamon

100 g (3½ oz) dried chillies, soaked and
**   ground separately**
¾ cup vinegar
3 cups water
6 tablespoons sugar
2 tablespoons salt
100 g (3½ oz) pickled small limes
150 g (5 oz) shallots | *peeled and*
100 g (3½ oz) garlic | *kept whole*
7½ cm (3 in) ginger, shredded
100 g (3½ oz) dried radish, cut into
**   1¼ cm (½ in) cubes**
60 g (2 oz) dried small sour starfruit
100 g (3½ oz) prunes
100 g (3½ oz) dried Chinese red dates
4 red chillies | *split lengthwise without*
4 green chillies | *cutting through*

2 tablespoons mustard seeds, roasted
2 tablespoons sesame seeds, roasted

Heat oil in a *kuali* and fry ground ingredients until fragrant then add ground chillies and fry till oil separates.

Put in vinegar, water, sugar and salt and bring to a slow boil. Simmer over low heat for 10 minutes until slightly thickened. Add pickled limes, shallots, garlic, shredded ginger, dried radish, small sour starfruit, prunes, red dates and red and green chillies.

Mix well and simmer over low heat for another 10 minutes. Just before removing from heat add mustard seeds and sesame seeds.

Note: To pickle small limes, boil 1½ cups vinegar with 240 g (8 oz) sugar and 2 tablespoons salt. Put in limes and when cooled keep in airtight jars for at least 2 weeks before using.

Kanji Kedah (Kedah Porridge)

Preparation: 15 minutes   Cooking: 1 hour

2 cups rice
8 cups water
240 g (8 oz) beef or chicken, cut into
**   thin strips**
240 g (8 oz) small prawns, shelled
2½ cm (1 in) ginger, shredded
1 stalk lemon grass, crushed lightly
1 teaspoon fenugreek
salt to taste
½ coconut, grated (for ¾ cup coconut
**   milk)**

Garnishing Ingredients
shallot crisps
spring onions, chopped
1 small head lettuce, sliced

Boil rice with 8 cups water over low heat for 40 minutes till grains are broken and porridge has a thick consistency. Put in beef or chicken, prawns, ginger, lemon grass and fenugreek. Bring to a slow boil and add salt to taste. Stir in coconut milk and when porridge boils again, remove from heat.

Serve hot, garnished with shallot crisps, spring onions and lettuce.

Ketupat Pulut

(photograph opposite)

Preparation: 30 minutes   Cooking: 2½ hours

**3 coconuts, grated (for 3½ cups
  thick coconut milk)**
1½ teaspoons salt
**1 kg (2¹/₅ lb) glutinous rice, washed and
  drained**
**10 pieces banana leaves, each 18 x 23 cm
  (7 x 9 in), scalded**

Put thick coconut milk and salt in a large saucepan and bring to a slow boil over low heat. Add
glutinous rice and stir for 10-15 minutes until
almost dry.

Cover saucepan and cook over low heat for 20
minutes until glutinous rice is half-cooked. Cool.

Put 3-4 tablespoons of half-cooked glutinous rice
in the centre of each banana leaf. Roll into a long
roll approximately 4 cm (1½ in) in diameter. Twist
and tie the two ends securely with strong string or
triple strength nylon threads. Secure roll by tying
string around the centre as well.

Place glutinous rice rolls in a steamer and steam
for 2 hours over low heat. Cool, discard banana
leaves and cut into 2½ cm (1 in) thick slices. Serve
with Serunding Daging (page 165).

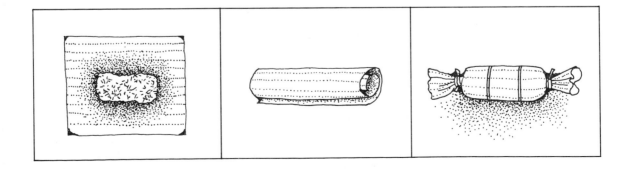

Opposite: Ketupat Pulut with Serunding Daging, Kedah Style

Mee Kedah

Preparation: 25 minutes   Cooking: 30 minutes

600 g (1⅓ lb) fresh yellow noodles
1 tablespoon oil
300 g (10 oz) beef, cut into thin strips
6 cups water
4 tablespoons oil

Ground Ingredients
20 dried chillies, soaked
8 shallots
3 cloves garlic

120 g (4 oz) dried prawns, ground
   separately
300 g (10 oz) small prawns, shelled
½ can (285 g/10 oz) condensed
   tomato soup
1 teaspoon monosodium glutamate
salt to taste
300 g (10 oz) mustard green, cut into 5 cm
   (2 in) lengths (separate stems and leaves)

Garnishing Ingredients
4 hardboiled eggs
2 firm soybean cakes, fried and cut into
   thick slices
300 g (10 oz) beansprouts, tailed
2 tomatoes, sliced
shallot crisps
spring onions ⎫
Chinese celery ⎬ *chopped*
5 red chillies, sliced

Scald noodles in boiling water, drain and mix with 1 tablespoon oil to prevent noodles from sticking. Place on a large serving dish.

Boil beef in water until beef is tender. Heat 4 tablespoons oil in a pot and fry ground ingredients for a few minutes, add dried prawns and fry until fragrant and crisp.

Pour in the beef and stock and bring to a boil. Add prawns, condensed tomato soup, monosodium glutamate and salt to taste. Put in vegetable, stems first. When cooked, pour over noodles.

Garnish with garnishing ingredients.

Laksa Kedah

Preparation: 1 hour Cooking: 30-35 minutes Serves: 10 approximately

600 g (1⅓ lb) fresh thick rice vermicelli
1¼ kg (2¾ lb) mackerel
12 cups water

Ground Ingredients
40 dried chillies, soaked
25 shallots
5 x 1¼ cm (2 x ½ in) dried shrimp paste

6 pieces dried tamarind skin
3 stalks wild ginger flowers, buds split and stems crushed lightly
2 small bunches polygonum leaves
a few sprigs mint leaves
450 g (1 lb) small prawns, shelled
salt to taste

Garnishing Ingredients
6 hardboiled eggs
2 onions, sliced finely
1 cucumber, shredded
½ head lettuce, shredded
5 red chillies, sliced
mint leaves

Scald thick rice vermicelli in boiling water for 3-4 minutes and drain well.

Steam fish for 12 minutes. Remove the flesh and blend fish bones with 3 cups of water. Pour into a saucepan and bring to a slow boil, then simmer for 10 minutes. Strain stock into an earthen pot.

Blend fish with a little water. Pour into the earthen pot together with remaining water. Add ground ingredients, dried tamarind skin, wild ginger flowers, polygonum and mint leaves and bring to a slow boil. Simmer gently for 20-25 minutes, then add prawns and salt to taste.

To serve, put a little vermicelli into individual serving bowls. Garnish with a little of each garnishing ingredient and pour gravy over. Serve hot.

PERLIS

Perlis, the smallest state in Peninsular Malaysia, abuts the Thai border. The State capital of Kangar is surrounded by limestone hills.

In this region, curry dishes cooked with lots of coconut milk — like Gulai Daging and Kurma Daging — are all-time favourites. They make tasty use of local ingredients and, though spicy, are delectable and simple to prepare.

Opposite: Kobis Masak Putih

Kari Kepala Ikan Jenahak

Preparation: 20 minutes   Cooking: 30 minutes

1 kg (2¹/₅ lb) 'jenahak' fish head
1 teaspoon salt
4 tablespoons oil
4 shallots ⎤
3 cloves garlic ⎦ *sliced*
½ teaspoon black peas
½ teaspoon fennel
½ teaspoon mustard seeds
1 teaspoon fenugreek
3 stalks curry leaves

Ground Ingredients
30 dried chillies, soaked
1 tablespoon coriander
1 dessertspoon cummin
2 teaspoons black peppercorns
1¼ cm (½ in) turmeric root
10 shallots
4 cloves garlic

1 coconut, grated (for 1 cup thick
   coconut milk and 2 cups thin
   coconut milk)

1 tablespoon tamarind paste ⎤ *mixed and*
½ cup water ⎦ *strained*
2 eggplants, cut at a slant into thick slices
1 teaspoon salt
½ teaspoon monosodium glutamate

Rub fish head with salt and leave for 15 minutes.

Heat oil in a *kuali* and fry sliced shallots and garlic, black peas, spices and curry leaves until fragrant.

Add ground ingredients and fry until fragrant and oil separates. Pour in thin coconut milk and tamarind juice and bring to a slow boil. Add eggplants and simmer for 5 minutes.

Put in fish head and cook over low heat for 12-15 minutes. Lastly, add thick coconut milk, salt and monosodium glutamate and bring to a slow boil, stirring gently.

Gulai Daging

Preparation: 20 minutes   Cooking: 45 minutes

600 g (1⅓ lb) beef
5 tablespoons oil
1 onion ⎤
3 cloves garlic ⎦ *sliced*
1¼ cm (½ in) stick cinnamon
2 sections of a star anise

Ground Ingredients
30 dried chillies, soaked
12 shallots
3 cloves garlic
2½ cm (1 in) ginger
2½ cm (1 in) turmeric root
1 heaped teaspoon fennel
1 teaspoon cummin
1 teaspoon black peppercorns
1¼ cm (½ in) stick cinnamon
3 sections of a star anise
3 cardamoms

1 coconut, grated (for 1 cup thick coconut
   milk and 2½ cups thin coconut milk)
3 potatoes, cut into wedges
1 teaspoon salt
½ teaspoon monosodium glutamate

Cut beef into thin slices.

Heat oil in a *kuali* and fry sliced ingredients and spices until fragrant. Add ground ingredients and fry over low heat until fragrant and oil separates.

Put in beef, stir-fry for 5 minutes, then pour in thin coconut milk. Simmer for 15 minutes. Add potatoes and cook till meat is tender and potatoes soft. Add thick coconut milk, salt and monosodium glutamate. Bring to a slow boil, stirring gently.

Kurma Daging Perlis

Preparation: 20 minutes   Cooking: 45 minutes

600 g (1 ⅓ lb) beef, sliced thinly
3 tablespoons kurma curry powder

Ground Ingredients
10 shallots
5 cloves garlic
2½ cm (1 in) galingale
2½ cm (1 in) ginger
1¼ cm (½ in) turmeric root
3 stalks lemon grass, sliced
1 teaspoon black peppercorns
4 tablespoons freshly grated white coconut

1 cup oil
4 shallots
2 cloves garlic } *sliced*
2½ cm (1 in) ginger
3 sections of a star anise
3 cloves
1¼ cm (½ in) stick cinnamon
1 coconut, grated (for 1 cup thick coconut milk and 4 cups thin coconut milk)
1 large piece dried tamarind skin
2 onions, quartered
1½ teaspoons salt

Slice beef thinly across the grain. Marinate with kurma curry powder and ground ingredients and leave for 15 minutes.

Heat oil in a *kuali* and fry sliced ingredients and spices until fragrant. Add beef and fry for a few minutes, then pour in thin coconut milk. Add tamarind skin and bring to a slow boil. Lower heat and simmer till meat is almost tender. Put in onion wedges and salt. Add thick coconut milk and simmer for another 5 minutes.

Note: For kenduris, *the beef is not sliced thinly but cut into fairly large pieces, each about 150 g (5 oz) in weight. Each piece is scored lightly, then boiled over low heat until almost tender.*

Rendang Ayam

Preparation: 20 minutes   Cooking: 30 minutes

1½ kg (3⅓ lb) chicken, cut into small pieces

Ground Ingredients
30 dried chillies, soaked
15 shallots
4 cloves garlic
2½ cm (1 in) ginger
2½ cm (1 in) turmeric root
1 teaspoon black peppercorns

1 tablespoon tamarind paste | *mixed and*
1 cup water | *strained*
2 tablespoons light soy sauce
1 teaspoon salt
7 tablespoons oil
2 stalks lemon grass, crushed lightly

Marinate chicken with ground ingredients, tamarind juice, light soy sauce and salt and leave for 30 minutes.

Heat oil in a *kuali* and fry lemon grass until fragrant. Put in chicken and fry over moderate heat for 5 minutes. Lower heat and simmer, covered, stirring occasionally, until chicken is tender and gravy is quite dry.

Gulai Ayam

Preparation: 20 minutes   Cooking: 40 minutes

1½ kg (3⅓ lb) chicken, cut into bite-size
   pieces
1 teaspoon salt
5 tablespoons oil
4 shallots ⎫
2 cloves garlic   ⎬ *sliced*
2½ cm (1 in) ginger ⎭
2 sections of a star anise
2 cloves
1¼ cm (½ in) stick cinnamon

Ground Ingredients
30 dried chillies, soaked
1 tablespoon coriander
1 teaspoon fennel
½ teaspoon cummin
10 shallots
2 cloves garlic
2½ cm (1 in) turmeric root

1 coconut, grated (for 1 cup thick coconut
   milk and 3 cups thin coconut milk)
1 teaspoon salt

Marinate chicken with salt and leave for 15 minutes.

Heat oil in a *kuali* and fry sliced ingredients and spices until fragrant. Add ground ingredients and fry until fragrant and oil separates. Put in chicken and stir-fry for 3 minutes, then add thin coconut milk. Simmer over low heat until meat is tender. Add thick coconut milk and salt and simmer for another 5 minutes.

Kerabu Taugeh with Tripe or Cockles

Preparation: 30 minutes   Cooking: 1 hour

600 g (1⅓ lb) tripe
1 teaspoon lime paste
2½ cm (1 in) ginger, crushed lightly
    or
1 kg (2⅕ lb) cockles
600 g (1⅓ lb) beansprouts, tailed

Ground Ingredients
6 red chillies, ground coarsely
2½ cm (1 in) ginger
3 stalks lemon grass
2 slices galingale
2½ cm (1 in) square dried shrimp paste,
   toasted
1 teaspoon black peppercorns

60 g (2 oz) rice, roasted in a dry pan till
   lightly browned and ground separately
2 onions, sliced finely
1 teaspoon tamarind paste ⎫ *mixed and*
2 tablespoons water   ⎭ *strained*

1½ teaspoons salt
½ white coconut, grated for 'kerisik'
½ coconut, grated (for 'pati santan')

Wash tripe and rub with lime paste. Rinse well. Put tripe and ginger in a saucepan with enough water to cover and boil over low heat for 1 hour until tripe is tender, or pressure cook for 30 minutes. Drain and when cool cut into thin slices. If using cockles, scald in boiling hot water and remove flesh from the shells.

Scald beansprouts in boiling water for a minute. Drain well and combine with tripe or cockles.

Add ground ingredients, ground rice, onions, tamarind juice, salt and *kerisik*. Just before serving add *pati santan*.

Kobis or Taugeh Masak Putih

(photograph on page 173)

Preparation: 10 minutes   Cooking: 15 minutes

300 g (10 oz) cabbage or beansprouts, tailed
½ coconut, grated (for ½ cup thick coconut milk and 4 cups thin coconut milk)
5 red chillies
6 shallots } *sliced*
1 clove garlic
300 g (10 oz) small prawns, shelled
½ teaspoon salt
¼ teaspoon monosodium glutamate
1 stalk spring onion, chopped

Cut cabbage into 1¼ cm (½ in) pieces.

Put thin coconut milk and sliced ingredients in a *kuali* and bring to a slow boil. Simmer for 5 minutes then add cabbage. When cabbage is soft, add prawns and thick coconut milk, salt and monosodium glutamate. Add spring onion last.

If using beansprouts, put in prawns, then add beansprouts and thick coconut milk. Remove from heat as soon as it comes to a boil.

Tepung Bungkus

Preparation: 30 minutes   Cooking: 30 minutes

240 g (8 oz) rice flour
2 cups water
1 coconut, grated (for 3 cups coconut milk)
210 g (7 oz) sugar
2 screwpine leaves, knotted
¼ teaspoon salt
16 banana leaves, cut into 18 x 15 cm (7 x 6 in) pieces, scalded

Filling
90 g (3 oz) palm sugar, chopped
½ cup water
180 g (6 oz) grated young coconut
¼ teaspoon salt

Sift rice flour into a bowl, add water and blend mixture until smooth.

Place coconut milk, sugar, screwpine leaves and salt in a saucepan over low heat and stir to dissolve sugar. Add rice batter and stir with a wooden spoon for approximately 5 minutes until mixture is cooked and turns into a smooth paste. Remove from heat.

Place a dessertspoonful of cooked dough mixture in the centre of each banana leaf. Fold one side of banana leaf over to flatten dough into a small rectangle. Place two marble-size balls of filling in the centre, about 1¼ cm (½ in) apart. Place another dessertspoonful of dough mixture on top of coconut filling. Fold banana leaf to overlap lengthwise over mixture and tuck the other ends under. Repeat with remaining dough and filling.

Steam for 20 minutes. Serve hot or cold.

Filling
Put palm sugar and water in a small saucepan and cook over low heat, stirring until sugar dissolves. Strain.

Place strained syrup in a *kuali* together with grated coconut and salt and fry till evenly coated with palm syrup. Dish out and cool. Form into marble-size balls.

SABAH & SARAWAK

Sabah and Sarawak form the States of East Malaysia. Compared with the other Malaysian States, Sabah is sparsely populated but is extremely rich in natural resources like timber and oil. Popularly known as the 'land below the wind', the world's oldest jungles offering a colourful profusion of exotic tropical flora and fauna are found there. Ibans form the largest indigenous group. These hardworking people live in communal longhouses throughout the jungles.

Sarawak, the land of the hornbills, has its capital, Kuching, perched on the banks of the Sarawak River. On the south shore lie the business district and port facilities, characterised by Chinese shophouses. The north shore is predominantly populated by Malays. Their lifestyle evolves along water villages of wooden houses rather precariously perched on stilts above the tidal Sarawak River.

The range of cuisine offered to the adventurous person is mainly Malay and Chinese, with superb fresh seafood. Malay cuisine is simple but remarkably tasty. Dried shrimp paste is a popular ingredient and moderately used for sweetness and flavour. Cakes are extremely popular, particularly steamed cakes which are very rich and the main attraction during festive occasions.

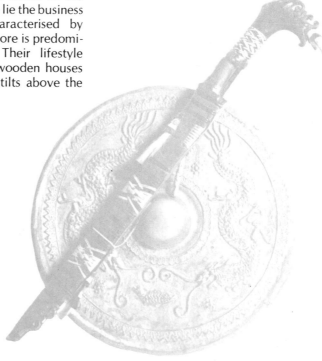

Opposite: Udang Masak Merah

Umai (Raw Fish Sambal)

Preparation: 15 minutes

300 g (10 oz) small threadfin
8 ripe 'asam paya'/'asam kelubi', hard
outer skin and seed removed
30 bird chillies, ground
8 shallots, sliced
4 cloves garlic, sliced
2½ cm (1 in) ginger, chopped
1 teaspoon salt
½ teaspoon monosodium glutamate

Wash and debone fish. Cut into thin slices. Chop *asam paya* and combine with ground bird chillies, sliced ingredients and chopped ginger.

Marinate fish with combined ingredients, salt and monosodium glutamate. Let it stand for 10 minutes before serving with boiled rice and one or two other dishes.

Sambal Santan Udang

Preparation: 20 minutes   Cooking: 10 minutes

600 g (1⅓ lb) medium prawns
6 tablespoons oil

Ground Ingredients
10 red chillies
2 onions
4 cloves garlic
4 stalks lemon grass
2½ cm (1 in) ginger
2½ cm (1 in) turmeric root
1¼ cm (½ in) square dried shrimp paste

½ coconut, grated (for 1¼ cups coconut milk)
1 heaped dessertspoon tamarind paste ⎤ *mixed and*
¼ cup water ⎦ *strained*
1 heaped teaspoon salt

Wash and clean prawns. Remove shells but leave tails on.

Heat oil and fry ground ingredients until fragrant and oil appears on surface. Add coconut milk and bring to a slow boil. Put in prawns, tamarind juice and salt to taste. Simmer for 5 minutes until prawns are cooked.

Udang Masak Merah

(photograph on page 178)

Preparation: 10 minutes   Cooking: 10 minutes

**1 kg (2¹/₅ lb) freshwater prawns ('udang
  galah' or king prawns)**
2 teaspoons salt
½ teaspoon pepper
1 ⅓ cups oil

Ground Ingredients
30-35 dried chillies, soaked
12 shallots
8 cloves garlic
4 cm (1½ in) galingale
2½ cm (1 in) square dried shrimp paste

4 tomatoes, quartered
1 teaspoon salt
1 teaspoon sugar

Clean prawns and trim off sharp ends of feelers and legs. Leave the shells intact. Marinate prawns with salt and pepper and leave for 30 minutes.

Heat oil in a *kuali* and fry ground ingredients over low heat until fragrant. Put in prawns, increasing heat at the same time. Stir-fry prawns, then add tomatoes. Sprinkle in a little water if it is too dry. Add salt and sugar. When the prawns turn bright red, they are cooked.

Rendang Daging

Preparation: 15 minutes   Cooking: 2 hours

**600 g (1⅓ lb) beef, cut into 4 cm (1½ in)
  thin slices**

Ground Ingredients
20 dried chillies, soaked
10 shallots
3 stalks lemon grass
2½ cm (1 in) galingale
2½ cm (1 in) ginger
2½ cm (1 in) turmeric root

**1 coconut, grated (for 4 cups
  coconut milk)**
1½ teaspoons salt

Put beef, ground ingredients and coconut milk in a pot and simmer, uncovered, for 2 hours until meat is tender and gravy is of a thick consistency. Add salt to taste.

Ayam Masak Asam Pedas

(photograph opposite)

Preparation: 20 minutes   Cooking: 30 minutes

1½ kg (3⅓ lb) chicken, cut into bite-size
    pieces
1 teaspoon salt
1 cup oil

Ground Ingredients
25 dried chillies, soaked
10 shallots
6 cloves garlic
3 candlenuts
2½ cm (1 in) ginger
2½ cm (1 in) galingale
1 stalk lemon grass
2 tablespoons coriander powder
1 teaspoon turmeric powder

1 coconut, grated (for 3 cups coconut
    milk)
2 cans (each 567 g/20 oz) pineapple cubes
1½ teaspoons salt

Marinate chicken with salt and leave for 30 minutes.

Heat oil and fry ground ingredients until fragrant and oil separates. Put in chicken and fry for 2 minutes. Add coconut milk and bring to a slow boil. Add pineapple cubes and simmer for 20 minutes until chicken is tender. Add salt to taste.

Ayam Masak Putih

Preparation: 15 minutes   Cooking: 20 minutes

½ chicken, about 1 kg (2⅕ lb), cut into
    bite-size pieces
1 teaspoon salt
4 tablespoons oil

Ground Ingredients
6 shallots
4 cloves garlic
2½ cm (1 in) ginger
2½ cm (1 in) galingale
½ tablespoon white peppercorns
½ tablespoon black peppercorns

½ coconut, grated (for 1 cup thick
    coconut milk and 2 cups thin coconut
    milk)
2 tomatoes, quartered
½ teaspoon salt

Season chicken with salt and leave for 30 minutes.

Heat oil in a *kuali* and fry ground ingredients until fragrant and oil separates. Put in chicken and fry for 2-3 minutes. Add thin coconut milk and bring to a boil. Add tomatoes and simmer for 15 minutes until chicken is tender. Add thick coconut milk and salt to taste.

Opposite: Ayam Masak Asam Pedas

Ayam Masak Kicap

Preparation: 15 minutes   Cooking: 25 minutes

½ **chicken, about 1 kg (2¹/₅ lb), cut into
  bite-size pieces**
1 **teaspoon salt**
½ **dessertspoon Allspice**
½ **tablespoon dark soy sauce**
5 **tablespoons oil**

Ground Ingredients
6 **shallots**
4 **cloves garlic**
2½ **cm (1 in) ginger**
½ **tablespoon black peppercorns**
½ **tablespoon white peppercorns**

³/₄ **cup water**
2 **onions, sliced**
2 **red chillies, sliced**
½ **teaspoon salt**

Season chicken with salt, Allspice, dark soy sauce and leave for 1 hour.

Heat oil and fry ground ingredients until fragrant. Put in chicken and fry for 3 minutes. Add water and bring to a boil. Simmer gently, covered, for 15 minutes until chicken is tender. Put in onions and chillies and stir-fry until gravy is thick. Add salt to taste.

Taugeh Tumis

Preparation: 10 minutes   Cooking: 5 minutes

4 **tablespoons oil**
2 **shallots** ⎫
1 **clove garlic** ⎭ *sliced*

Ground Ingredients
½ **cup (30 g/1 oz) dried anchovies,
  heads and entrails removed**
1¼ **cm (½ in) square dried shrimp paste**

2 **firm soybean cakes, cut into 1¼ cm
  (½ in) cubes**
300 **g (10 oz) beansprouts, tailed**
12 **stalks Chinese chives, cut into 4 cm
  (1½ in) lengths**
½ **teaspoon salt**
1 **red chilli, sliced**

Heat oil in a *kuali* and lightly brown shallots and garlic. Add ground ingredients and fry over low heat until fragrant. Add soybean cakes, increasing heat at the same time. Stir-fry, sprinkling in a little water if it is too dry. Put in beansprouts and stir-fry for 1 minute. Add Chinese chives, salt and red chilli and stir-fry quickly to mix ingredients. Serve hot.

Bubur Pedas

Preparation: 30 minutes   Cooking: 30 minutes

120 g (4 oz) rice, washed and drained
90 g (3 oz) grated coconut
3 shallots
2 cloves garlic
5 dried chillies, soaked and
  seeded
1 stalk lemon grass   } *chopped*
2½ cm (1 in) ginger
2½ cm (1 in) galingale
2½ cm (1 in) turmeric root
2 cups water
3 tablespoons oil
2 shallots   } *sliced*
1 clove garlic
1 tablespoon coriander
½ dessertspoon cummin
½ dessertspoon fennel   } *roasted and*
1¼ cm (½ in) stick cinnamon   *ground finely*
4 sections of a star anise
1 cardamom
½ coconut, grated (for 1 cup thick
  coconut milk and 3 cups thin coconut
  milk)
300 g (10 oz) small prawns or beef, cut into
  small pieces
4 dried Chinese mushrooms, soaked and
  diced
45 g (1½ oz) soybean sticks, soaked and
  cut into small pieces
2 heaped teaspoons salt

Put rice, grated coconut and chopped ingredients into a *kuali* and roast over low heat for 10 minutes or until fragrant and lightly browned. Place in a blender and blend with 2 cups water. Leave to soak for 20 minutes. (Or pound the roasted ingredients until fine then soak in 2 cups water.)

Heat oil in a pot and lightly brown shallots and garlic. Put in rice mixture, ground spices and thin coconut milk and bring to a slow boil, stirring frequently. Add meat, mushrooms, soybean sticks and bring to a boil again. Simmer for 5 minutes then add thick coconut milk and salt to taste.

Note: Bubur Pedas is popular with the Muslims in Sarawak especially during the fasting month. Prepared Bubur Pedas ingredients are readily available in small packets.

Kek Masam Manis

(photograph opposite)

Preparation: 20 minutes   Steaming: 42 minutes

5 eggs, separated
150 g (5 oz) castor sugar
250 g (8½ oz) butter
½ can (397 g/10 oz) condensed milk
1 teaspoon vanilla essence
150 g (5 oz) soda crackers, milled or
   pounded and sifted
¼ teaspoon green colouring
15 packets Haw Flakes

Note: Haw Flakes are thin red flakes the size of a 20 cent coin. Made in China and sold in most local sweet shops, they are sweet-and-sour and favourites with most children.

Whisk egg whites until stiff, then gradually add sugar a spoonful at a time, beating well after each addition.

In a separate bowl, cream butter, condensed milk and vanilla essence until light and fluffy. Add egg yolks one at a time, beating well after each addition.

Add egg yolk mixture to egg white mixture. Combine lightly and evenly. Fold in milled crackers and divide mixture into two equal portions. Colour one portion green.

Line the base of a 21 cm (8½ in) round cake tin with greased greaseproof paper. Spread a third of the green mixture evenly onto base of lined tin. Arrange 3 packets of Haw Flakes on the surface. Steam over rapid boiling water for 7 minutes. Remove from steamer and spread a third of the yellow mixture over steamed layer. Arrange 3 packets of Haw Flakes on top and resteam for 7 minutes. Repeat procedure alternating layers with remaining mixtures and Haw Flakes.

Allow cake to cool in the tin for 15 minutes before turning out onto a wire rack. Cool thoroughly before cutting.

Kek Cream Soda

Preparation: 15 minutes   Baking: 35 minutes   Oven setting: 175°C, 350°F, Gas Regulo 6

180 g (6 oz) butter
3 large eggs
90 g (3 oz) castor sugar
1 teaspoon vanilla or lemon essence
240 g (8 oz) flour | *sifted*
1 teaspoon baking powder |
1 cup ice cream soda

Beat butter until light and creamy. In a separate bowl whisk eggs and castor sugar until light and fluffy. Stir in beaten butter and essence. Carefully fold in sifted flour and baking powder alternately with ice cream soda.

Pour mixture into a 21 cm (8½ in) round cake tin lined with greased greaseproof paper. Bake in a moderate oven for 35 minutes or until cooked when tested with a skewer.

Opposite: Kek Masam Manis

Madu Kemeyan

Preparation: 20 minutes   Steaming: 40 minutes

250 g (8½ oz) butter
180 g (6 oz) castor sugar
1 tablespoon brown sugar
5 eggs, separated
120 g (4 oz) Horlicks
60 g (2 oz) soda crackers, milled or
    pounded and sifted
2 tablespoons cocoa, sifted
1 tablespoon golden syrup
3 tablespoons condensed milk
90 g (3 oz) flour, sifted

Cream half the butter with 60 g (2 oz) of the castor sugar and brown sugar until light and fluffy. Add egg yolks one at a time, beating well after each addition. Stir in Horlicks, soda crackers, cocoa and golden syrup.

In a separate bowl, cream remaining butter with condensed milk until light and fluffy.

In another bowl, whisk egg whites until stiff. Gradually beat in remaining 120 g (4 oz) of the castor sugar, a spoonful at a time, beating well after each addition. Stir in butter and condensed milk mixture. Carefully fold in sifted flour and mix well.

Line the base of a 21 cm (8½ in) round cake tin with greased greaseproof paper. Spread 7-8 dessertspoonfuls of the egg white mixture evenly over base of lined tin. Steam over rapid boiling water for 8 minutes until cake is firm to the touch. Remove from steamer. Drop alternate spoonfuls of egg white and chocolate mixture 1¼ cm (½ in) apart over surface of steamed cake. Resteam for 10 minutes. Repeat procedure with both remaining mixtures. Allow cake to cool in tray for 15 minutes before turning out onto a wire rack to cool completely.

Kek Kukus Sri Kaya

Preparation: 15 minutes   Steaming: 50 minutes

180 g (6 oz) butter
150 g (5 oz) castor sugar
4 tablespoons evaporated milk
4 tablespoons egg jam ('kaya')
1 tablespoon golden syrup
1 teaspoon vanilla essence
5 large egg yolks
180 g (6 oz) flour ⎫ sifted
1 teaspoon baking powder ⎭
a few drops green colouring

Cream butter and sugar until light and fluffy then beat in evaporated milk, egg jam, golden syrup and vanilla essence. Add egg yolks one at a time and beat well. Fold in sifted flour and mix well.

Divide mixture into two equal portions. Stir green colouring into one portion. Grease a 20 cm (8 in) round cake tin with butter and spread half the green batter into tin. Spread out evenly and smoothen with the back of a spoon. Repeat layers, alternating colours. Place in a steamer over rapid boiling water and steam for 50 minutes.

Carefully turn out onto a wire rack to cool before cutting.

Kek Embun Pagi

Preparation: 20 minutes   Steaming: 45 minutes

250 g (8½ oz) butter
150 g (5 oz) castor sugar
8 eggs, separated
³/₄ can (397 g/10 oz) condensed milk
¼ teaspoon almond essence
240 g (8 oz) flour ⎫
1 teaspoon baking powder ⎬ *sifted*
a few drops green colouring
a few drops yellow colouring (if desired)
a few drops red colouring
60 g (2 oz) almond flakes
120 g (4 oz) castor sugar
1 teaspoon vanilla essence
150 g (5 oz) flour, sifted
10 red cherries, sliced

Cream butter and sugar until light and fluffy. Add egg yolks one at a time, beating well after each addition. Add condensed milk and almond essence and cream further until light and creamy. Fold in sifted flour and baking powder, half at a time.

Divide mixture into three equal parts. Into one, blend a few drops of green colouring. Leave the second plain or blend in a few drops of yellow colouring. Into the third, blend a few drops of red colouring.

Line a 25 cm (10 in) round cake tin with greased greaseproof paper. Spoon in green mixture and spread evenly. Steam over rapid boiling water for 10 minutes until cake is firm to the touch. Remove from steamer and sprinkle half of the almond flakes over cake. Spread yellow mixture over this and steam for another 10 minutes. Repeat procedure with remaining almond flakes and red mixture.

Whisk egg whites until just stiff. Gradually beat in sugar half at a time, beating well after each addition. Add vanilla essence. Carefully fold in sifted flour and mix well. Spoon egg white mixture over steamed cake and spread evenly and smoothly. Arrange cherry slices on top and steam again for 12 minutes.

Allow cake to cool in tin for 15 minutes before turning out onto a wire rack to cool completely.

Glossary

Ingredients

English	Malay/Local
Abalone/oyster mushroom	Cendawan abalon/tiram
Alkaline water	Air alkali
	Kan sui
Almond	Biji buah badam
Anchovy	Ikan bilis
Bamboo shoot	Rebung
Banana leaf	Daun pisang
Basil	Daun kemangi,
	Daun selasih
Beansprout	Taugeh
Beef	Daging lembu
Bird chilli	Cili padi
Bittergourd	Peria
Black peas	Kacang hitam
Black peppercorns	Lada hitam
Black pomfret	Ikan bawal hitam
Black shrimp paste	Petis
	Heiko
Black sweet sauce	Kicap hitam manis
Borax	Pangsar
Brown sugar	Gula merah
Butter	Mentega
Button mushroom	Cendawan butang

English	Malay/Local
Cabbage	Kobis
Candlenut	Buah keras
Cardamom	Buah pelaga
Carrot	Lobak merah
Cashew nut	Biji gajus
Cashewnut leaf	Daun gajus
Catfish	Ikan sembilang
Cauliflower	Bunga kobis
Cekur leaves	Daun cekur
Chicken	Ayam
Chinese celery	Daun sup
	Selderi
Chinese chives	Kucai
Chinese red dates	Korma Cina
Cinnamon	Kulit kayu manis
Cloud ear fungus	Telinga tikus
Cloves	Bunga cengkih
Cockle	Kerang
Coconut	Kelapa
Coconut milk	Santan
Coconut milk residue	Tahi minyak (Johore)
	Minyak muda (Pahang)
Coconut milk, thick	Pati santan
Condensed milk	Susu pekat
Coriander	Ketumbar

English	Malay/Local	English	Malay/Local
Coriander leaves	Daun ketumbar	Horse mackerel	Ikan selar kuning
Crab	Ketam		Ikan cencaru
Crab roe	Telur ketam		
Cucumber	Timun	Jackfruit leaf	Daun nangka
Cummin	Jintan putih		
Curry leaf	Daun kari	*Kaduk* leaf	Daun kaduk
Cuttlefish	Sotong		
		Lady's fingers	Bendi
Dark soy sauce	Kicap hitam	Large/big lime	Limau nipis
Double lime leaf	Daun limau perut	Leek	Daun bawang Cina
Dried chilli	Lada/cili kering	Lemon grass	Serai
Dried Chinese mushroom	Cendawan kering Cina	Lentil	Dal/dhal
Dried cuttlefish	Sotong kering	Lettuce	Daun salad
Dried fish bladder	Pundi kering ikan	Light soy sauce	Kicap putih
Dried prawns	Udang kering	Long bean	Kacang panjang
Dried radish	Lobak asin		
	Caipo	Mace	Bunga pala
Dried shrimp paste	Belacan	Mackerel	Ikan kembung
Dried tamarind skin	Asam gelugur	Malt	Mak gar tong
Duck	Itik	Mint leaf	Daun pudina
		Monosodium glutamate	Serbuk perasa
Egg	Telur	Mustard greens	Sawi
Eggplant	Terung	Mustard seed	Biji sawi
Evaporated milk	Susu cair	Mutton	Daging kambing
Fennel	Jintan manis	Nutmeg	Buah pala
Fenugreek	Halba		
Fermented durian	Tempoyak	Onion	Bawang besar
Firm soybean cake	Taukwa	Oyster sauce	Kicap tiram
Five-spice powder	Serbuk lima rempah		
Flat rice noodles	Kway teow	Palm sugar	Gula melaka
	Sar ho fun	Peanut candy	Bipang kacang
Flour	Tepung	Pepper	Serbuk lada
Freshwater prawns	Udang galah	*Petai*	Petai
		Pineapple	Nenas
Galingale	Lengkuas	Plum sauce	Kicap buah asam
Garlic	Bawang putih	Polygonum	Daun kesum
Garlic flakes	Bawang putih kering	Pomfret	Ikan bawal
Ginger	Halia	Poppy seed	Biji kas-kas
Glutinous rice	Pulut	Potato	Ubi kentang
Green chilli	Lada/cili hijau	Preserved/salted Tientsin	Sawi asin
Green pepper/Capsicum	Lada Jepun	cabbage	Kiamchye
Green beans	Kacang hijau	Preserved soy beans	Taucu
Green bean flour	Tepung kacang hijau	Preserved soybean cake	Tempe
Green peas	Kacang pis	Pumpkin	Labu
Green stems	Kai choy	Pumpkin leaf	Pucuk labu
Groundnuts	Kacang tanah	Prawn	Udang
Ground toasted coconut	Kerisik	Prune	Prun
Grouper	Kerapu, Garoupa		
Gypsum	Sekko		

English	Malay/Local	English	Malay/Local
Radish	Lobak Cina	Straw mushroom	Cendawan jerami
	Lobak putih	Sugar	Gula pasir
Raisins/sultanas	Kismis	Sultan fish	Ikan ketutu
Red chilli	Lada/cili kering		Soon hock yee
Red snapper	Ikan merah	Sweet potato	Ubi keledek
	Ikan jenahak		
	Hong cho yee	Tamarind paste	Asam jawa
Rice, cooked	Nasi	Tamarind skin	Asam gelugur
Rice, uncooked	Beras	Tapioca	Ubi kayu
Rice vermicelli	Mihun	Tapioca flour	Tepung sagu
	Bihun	Tapioca leaf	Pucuk ubi kayu
		Thick rice vermicelli	Laksa mihun
Saffron strands	Koma-koma	Threadfin	Ikan kurau
Salt	Garam	Tomato	Tomato
Saltfish	Ikan masin	Tomato puree	Tomato puri
Screwpine leaf	Daun pandan	Transparent noodles	Tunghoon
Sesame oil	Minyak bijan		Suun
Sesame seed	Bijan	Tripe	Perut lembu
	Lenga	Turmeric leaf	Daun kunyit
Shad	Ikan terubuk	Turmeric root	Kunyit hidup
Shallot	Bawang kecil	Turnip	Sengkuang
Sichuan peppercorns	Lada merah		
	Fah chew	Vinegar	Cuka
Small/local lime	Limau kasturi		
Small sour starfruit	Belimbing buluh	Water chestnut	Sengkuang Cina
Soda crackers	Biskut soda	Watercress	Daun penggaga
Soft soybean cake	Tauhu lembik	White peppercorns	Lada putih
Soybean skin	Kulit tauhu	Wild ginger flower	Bunga kantan
Soybean sprout	Taugeh besar	Wolf herring	Ikan parang
Spanish mackerel	Ikan tenggiri		
Spring onion	Daun bawang	Yam	Keladi
Star anise	Bunga lawang	Yellow noodles	Mi
	Buah pekkak	Yellow tailor	Ikan kuning

Opposite:
1 Mustard seeds
2 Mace
3 Cinnamon sticks
4 Saffron strands
5 Cashew nuts
6 Five-spice powder
7 Poppy seeds
8 Gypsum (sekko)
9 Candlenuts
10 Almonds

11 Sichuan peppercorns
12 Cardamoms
13 Nutmegs
14 Fenugreek
15 Star anise
16 Lentils
17 Coriander seeds
18 Dried chillies
19 Fennel
20 Toasted sesame seeds
21 Black peas

22 Soy beans
23 Black peppercorns
24 Shelled peanuts
25 Green beans
26 Cloves
27 Cummin
28 White peppercorns
29 'Nasi Dagang' rice
(not unpolished rice)
30 White polished rice
31 Glutinous rice

Your Ingredients at a Glance

1 Chinese celery
2 Small sour starfruit
3 Ginger
4 Basil leaves
5 Turmeric root
6 Curry leaves
7 Polygonum leaves
8 Big limes
9 Small limes
10 Preserved soybean cake
11 Button mushrooms
12 Haw flakes
13 Double lime leaves
14 Straw mushrooms
15 Chinese red dates
16 *Cekur* leaves
17 Mint leaves
18 Dried fish bladder
19 Dried fish bladder (fried)
20 Bird chillies
21 Cloud ear fungus
22 Dried tamarind skin
23 Dried cuttlefish
24 Dried cuttlefish flakes
25 Garlic
26 Soda crackers
27 Abalone/oyster mushrooms
28 Red chillies
29 Turmeric leaves
30 Dried radish
31 Lemon grass
32 Chinese chives
33 Wild ginger flower
34 Green chillies

35 Onions
36 Galingale
37 *Kaduk* leaves
38 Cashewnut leaves
39 Cashewnut fruit
40 Coriander leaves
41 Turnip
42 Preserved Tientsin cabbage
43 Mustard greens
44 Screwpine leaves
45 Spring onion
46 Leek
47 *Petai*
48 Jackfruit leaves
49 Yám
50 Green stems
51 Dried shrimp paste
52 Palm sugar
53 Sesame oil
54 Light soy sauce
55 Black sweet sauce
56 Dark soy sauce
57 Oyster sauce
58 Shallots
59 Preserved soy beans
60 Dried prawns
61 Soybean skin wrapper
62 Dried Chinese mushrooms
63 Peanut candy
64 Tamarind paste
65 Ground roasted coconut
66 Black shrimp paste
67 Preserved soy beans
68 Plum sauce

Kitchen Terms

This second glossary which includes words used to name the dishes in the book may be useful to those unfamiliar with Malay or local cooking terms. Many of them are descriptive.

Acar Fruits or vegetables pickled, usually in vinegar or some other acidic medium, such as lime juice.

Asam, masam Sour.

Bandung A town in West Java, Indonesia.

Berendam Soaked or immersed in liquid.

Berhias Embellished or decorated.

Berlauk *Lauk* means food eaten with rice, e.g. meat or fish; *berlauk* means 'with food'.

Bersantan Similarly, *bersantan* means (cooked) 'with *santan*' or coconut milk.

Betik Any edible fruit with yellow flesh, such as papaya (pawpaw).

Biryani Rice cooked with oil or ghee, coloured with saffron or the less costly turmeric, and flavoured with spices.

Bolu Usually *kuih bolu*, a light cake made with highly whipped eggs and sugar, flour folded in just before baking.

Botok A dish, usually of fish wrapped in vegetables or leaves and steamed with spices and coconut milk. Gulai Botok very likely describes the slow cooking process which is quite akin to steaming.

Bubur Soft porridge, of rice mixed with other food.

Bungkus Wrap, as in a bundle.

Cabai Chilli.

Dadar A kind of pancake.

Dalca An Indian dish made by boiling lentils (*dal*) with spices and sometimes meat and vegetables.

Debal/Devil A very hot curry.

Dinding A district in Perak.

Dodol A sticky sweet made of glutinous rice flour and coconut milk, sugar or palm sugar, and sometimes flavoured with local fruit like durian.

Embun pagi Mist or dew of the morning (*pagi*); in Kek Embun Pagi the words probably describe the cake's lightness.

Encik Kebin The origin of this one is a puzzle. *Encik* is a title whose English equivalent is 'Mister' and *Kebin* is 'cabin', as in a ship's cabin, but it could of course also be the name of the originator of this dish!

Garam Salt.

Golek Literally, roll over or lie flat. Combined with *ayam* (chicken), as in Ayam Golek, this refers to a chicken, usually cooked whole.

Goreng Fry, either in a dry pan or in oil.

Gulai Food cooked with gravy or sauce.

Jala Net, usually fishing net. Roti Jala refers to the net-like appearance of the *roti* (bread or pancake).

Jemput Or *jemput-jemput*, a cake made by deep-frying soft batter, usually of flour, sugar and fruit like banana or durian.

Kanji Starch, such as the liquid obtained after boiling rice in water for a long time.

Kapitan Captain; historically in Malaysia this word referred to a headman in a Chinese community.

Kari Curry.

Kek Cake.

Kemeyan Incense.

Kerabu A salad, usually of vegetables, but *kerabu* may describe any dish of ingredients (cooked or raw) tossed together salad fashion just before serving.

Kering Dry.

Kerutuk A dish, usually of chicken, cooked with spices till nearly dry.

Ketupat Sometimes *nasi ketupat*, this refers to rice cooked in a shell of coconut leaves to give a compressed rice cake eaten with a thick sauce or food with thick gravy. This compressed rice may take the form of *nasi himpit* (page 111), *ketupat pulut* (page 168) or even *lemang* (page 50).

Koleh-koleh A sweet made with ground or blended beans or tapioca. In Indonesia, *koleh-koleh* is used in reference to any sweet made by constant stirring in a to-and-fro motion.

Kuah lada Chilli hot gravy.

Kuih Any sweet food, like cake or sweatmeats.

Kuih bakar A cake made by baking, grilling or toasting.

Kuih cara A type of cake. *Cara* actually means way or method of doing.

Kuih lapis A layered cake or sweet; *lapis* means layers.

Kukus Steam.

Kurma A stew of meat or chicken with spices.

Laksa This refers both to thick rice vermicelli and to a dish of this in spicy coconut milk gravy.

Lawar Thin slices of meat or fish.

Lemak Fat or oily. Describes any rich oily dish, usually cooked in coconut milk.

Lodeh Vegetables cooked till soft in a coconut milk gravy.

Madu Honey or nectar.

Manis Sweet.

Masak Cook. The word *masak* is often followed by other words (as in *masak asam, masak keremak, masak kicap*) which merely describe the way the food is cooked. Hence, *masak merah* means cooked red and virtually describes the dish by colour.

Masam manis Sour sweet.

Nagasari A type of tree with white flowers. In food, a sweet made with steamed green bean flour batter and slices of banana.

Nasi kunyit Sometimes called Nasi Kuning (*kuning* = yellow), this is rice cooked with turmeric (*kunyit*) to give it an attractive colour.

Nasi ulam Rice eaten with *ulam* or raw vegetables, leaves or fruit.

Opor A rich dish of chic[...] seasoned thick coconut [...] appearance.

Otak-otak Usually fish [...] wrapped in coconut or b[...] steamed or toasted.

Panggang Roasted over li[...]

Pedas Chilli hot.

Pengantin Bride or groon[...]

Pengat A rich dessert of [...] tato, banana, etc., cooke[...] sugar.

Percik Splash, spatter, scatter.

Pincuk Several ingredients, cooked or raw, mixed salad fashion, just before serving. See also *Kerabu*.

Pindang A dish of seafood cooked in a sour soup.

Puding Pudding.

Puteri An elegant cake or sweet. *Puteri* literally means 'princess'.

Putih White.

Rampai Mixture or variety of things.

Rebus Boil.

Rembau A small town in Negri Sembilan.

Rempah Usually *rempah-rempah*, a ground mixture of spices.

Rendang Meat or chicken fried with spices and coconut milk till dry.

Rojak A salad of raw or preserved vegetables and fruit, served cold with a sauce.

Roti Bread, or any staple made with flour, like pancake.

Sambal Any food made with chillies and *rempah*.

Satay Marinated meat, skewered and barbequed, served on skewers with a sauce.

Semur Stew, usually of meat.

Serimuka Actually two words, *seri muka* or glowing face.

Serunding Flaked meat or fish cooked with spices and grated coconut.

Solo Literally solo, single, one.

Solok A gift of food brought to a feast.

Soto A spicy pepper-hot soup with beansprouts, [...] and shredded meat.

[...] *seri* means brilliant, glow[...] [...]yal honorific. *Kaya* means [...]as to be wonderful indeed [...]n.

[...]an jelly dessert, also known

[...]ly, always, again and again. [...]ce of the dish which brings [...] for it.

197

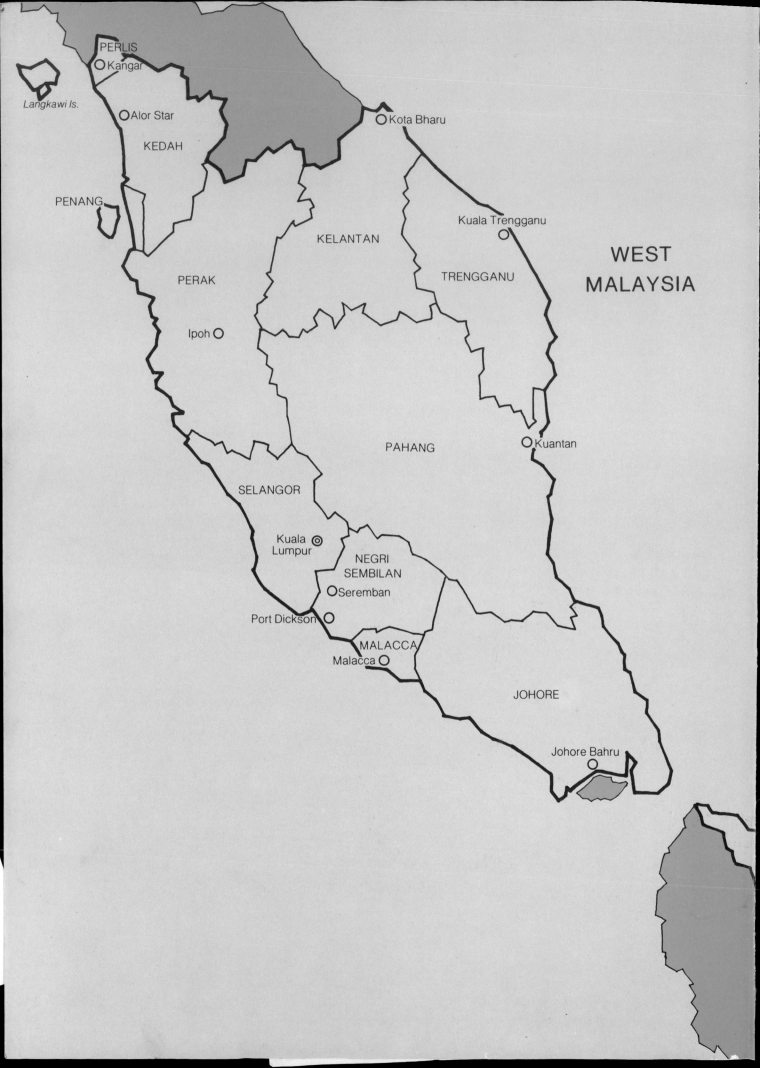